Connecting Across Disciplines

Other Titles by the Authors
Using Informational Text to Teach To Kill a Mockingbird
Using Informational Text to Teach A Raisin in the Sun

Connecting Across Disciplines

Collaborating with Informational Text

Audrey Fisch and Susan Chenelle

ROWMAN & LITTLEFIELD
Lanham • Boulder • New York • London

Published by Rowman & Littlefield
A wholly owned subsidiary of The Rowman & Littlefield Publishing Group, Inc.
4501 Forbes Boulevard, Suite 200, Lanham, Maryland 20706
www.rowman.com

Unit A, Whitacre Mews, 26-34 Stannary Street, London SE11 4AB

Copyright © 2016 by Rowman & Littlefield

All rights reserved. No part of this book may be reproduced in any form or by any electronic or mechanical means, including information storage and retrieval systems, without written permission from the publisher, except by a reviewer who may quote passages in a review.

British Library Cataloguing in Publication Information Available

Library of Congress Cataloging-in-Publication Data
Names: Chenelle, Susan, 1975- author. | Fisch, Audrey A., author.
Title: Connecting across disciplines : collaborating with informational text/ Susan Chenelle and Audrey Fisch.
Description: Lanham, Maryland : Rowman & Littlefield, 2016. | Includes bibliographical references.
Identifiers: LCCN 2015040971| ISBN 9781475820270 (cloth : alk. paper) |
    ISBN 9781475820287 (pbk. : alk. paper) | ISBN 9781475820294 (electronic)
Subjects: LCSH: Content area reading. | Reading (Elementary) | Reading comprehension—Study and teaching (Elementary) | Reading (Secondary) | Reading comprehension—Study and teaching (Elementary)
Classification: LCC LB1050.455 .C524 2016 | DDC 372.47/6—dc23 LC record available at http://lccn.loc.gov/2015040971

∞™ The paper used in this publication meets the minimum requirements of American National Standard for Information Sciences—Permanence of Paper for Printed Library Materials, ANSI/NISO Z39.48-1992.

Printed in the United States of America

Contents

Preface	vii
Acknowledgments	xi
Permissions	xiii
1 Literacy: Everyone's Responsibility (and Opportunity)	1
2 Collaboration: The Gift of the Common Core	11
3 Our Model for Finding and Using Great Informational Texts	21
4 Preparing an Informational Text	29
5 Making Vocabulary Work	33
6 Supporting Active Reading	45
7 Checking for Understanding	51
8 Extending Learning: Writing and Discussion Activities	61
9 Thinking Big: Class Activities and Projects	65
10 Using Hooks: Multimedia	71
11 Alignment with Common Core Assessments	77
12 You Can Do This: Keys to Implementation	83
Appendix A: The Fruit Fly Unit	91
Index	105
About the Authors	109

Preface

This volume is the product of collaboration. It started with Audrey's observation, based on her work with preservice and practicing English teachers, that teachers were worried about meeting the new informational text standard and Susan's agreement, based on her experience as an English teacher, that informational text offered an important opportunity for teachers to enhance their instruction. With all the hubbub in the media about the 70 percent mandate for informational text, we wanted, with our respective vantage points, to contribute to the emerging conversation about the implementation of the Common Core standards.

As educators, we were sympathetic to concerns about how the informational text standard would impact the teaching of literature, but we realized that using informational texts could both broaden student understanding of background and context for literary texts and deepen relevance by allowing students to make connections beyond the literary text with issues and ideas that impact their lives.

In our first book together on this project, *Using Informational Text to Teach To Kill a Mockingbird* (2014), we offer students the opportunity to read *Loving v. Virginia* in order to understand the broader context of Dolphus Raymond's interracial relationship. Scout and Jem know that Raymond's relationship represents a cultural taboo; reading an excerpt from *Loving v. Virginia*, our students can learn that an interracial marriage would have been illegal during the time of *Mockingbird* (Lee 1960) and long after.

In addition, we offer students the opportunity to think about the kind of work lawyers like Atticus do today and the challenges they continue to face in defending politically unpopular clients. An op-ed piece by a lawyer who defended Timothy McVeigh (Jones 2010) about the backlash against lawyers working to provide legal defense to the Guantanamo detainees lays out for students the ways in which Atticus's story is not some distant and irrelevant reality.

As we began to work with language arts teachers to take advantage of the opportunities afforded by informational text in connection with literature, we realized the opportunities for cross-disciplinary collaboration using informational text were equally exciting.

Informational texts in all content areas offer students the opportunity to see the larger context for what they're studying and why it matters. Relevant, timely informational texts have the potential to answer the "so what?" in every discipline and break down the artificial barriers between subjects and between school and the real world. In so doing, they offer content-area teachers in all disciplines opportunities to build interest, engagement, and motivation.

A unit built around the study of gendered aggression in fruit flies can connect with William Golding's *Lord of the Flies*, scientific research and methods, nature versus nurture in gendered behavior, and neuroscience. The possibilities for students to make connections begin to multiply exponentially.

Still, even as content-area teachers buy into the idea that these kinds of texts can increase student motivation and engagement, they worry about having the skills and time to design and implement meaningful lessons around them. Science teachers, for example, may be skeptical about how they can successfully incorporate articles or scientific studies into their teaching when their students struggle with their textbooks. In our workshops, we hear over and over again from content-area teachers of their concerns about teaching reading and how ill prepared they feel about helping students navigate the challenges of informational text: from challenging vocabulary to different text features.

We offer our model as a practical framework for language arts and content-area teachers to help each other and collaborate.

We begin, in chapter 1, with a discussion of how the shared responsibility for literacy is one of the great opportunities afforded by the Common Core.

In chapter 2, we talk about the possibilities and realities of collaboration. Start small; work with someone you like. Find a level of collaboration that works for you, your colleague, and the realities of your school setting; use and adapt the relevant elements of our model to get started.

In chapter 3, we review our model and discuss when to integrate an informational text into your curriculum and tips for finding timely, engaging, accessible texts. In chapter 4, we talk about the importance of excerpting your text to minimize distractions and challenges so as to maximize the text connection with your curriculum. Chapter 5 stresses the importance of tackling challenging vocabulary, and we offer a range of authentic vocabulary activities designed to build your students' language skills generally but particularly to front-load key terms and ideas so that your students are prepared to meet the challenges of your complex informational text.

Chapter 6 suggests a framework for building reading supports into your students' encounter with the informational text in a way that will support all learners. Because we think standardized assessment is an important reality in the world today, we offer models for both standardized assessments in chapter 7 and more in-depth and complex assessments in chapter 8.

For those teachers who want the informational text to form the basis for a large-scale reimagining of an existing unit in their curriculum, we offer ideas for class activities and projects in chapter 9.

In chapter 10, we discuss the importance of finding and using a variety of effective hooks, including multimedia, to build background knowledge and motivation around the subject of your informational text while also taking advantage of and supporting students' multimedia literacy.

For teachers who struggle with the challenges of standardized assessments, especially those who are regularly asked to set aside their curriculum in order to engage in test preparation, we offer chapter 11, which details the ways in which this model aligns with the tasks on common assessments, such as PARCC and Smarter Balanced. We hope the information in this chapter will allow you to make the argument that your test-preparation work is already integrated into your curriculum through your use of informational text in connection with your content area.

Finally, chapter 12 returns to the issue of challenges of collaboration and offers concrete suggestions and support about the practicalities of implementing this model in the classroom.

In the appendix, you will find a complete version of our *Lord of the Flies/* fruit fly unit. Answers for reference purposes, and editable versions of some of our organizers and rubrics are available at www.usinginformationaltext. org. The password to open the files is collaboration2016.

Our approach strives to help teachers feel confident in finding, preparing, and teaching informational text units—both for their own classrooms and in collaboration with colleagues—in an organic way that connects with their curriculum and their students. To be successful, teachers need to be fully comfortable with this process. These units can't be one-size-fits-all or set-it-and-forget-it. An informational text connection that may work well in one time at one school with one set of students may not work well in another setting.

Mastering the ability to create and teach a successful informational text unit gives teachers the opportunity to create fresh, relevant approaches to their existing curriculum on an ongoing basis. In this volume, we will show you how to find, prepare, and use informational texts in ways that enrich your curriculum and enhance student engagement and literacy.

We also offer, in chapter 2, "Collaboration," and chapter 12, "Keys to Implementation," suggestions for how to seize opportunities for creative, productive collaboration across content areas in your school. And we discuss the importance of different models of collaboration, with the reminder that small-scale collaborations can pay big dividends and ideas for how to begin and divide up the workload and the teaching for these kinds of collaborations.

Teaching is busy, labor-intensive work, and we all struggle to find enough hours in the day to do all we want to do with our curriculum and our students. Successful collaboration, however, can help us make the most of the time and effort we devote to our instruction.

As Meenoo Rami (2014) notes, "Look around any school that solves challenges collaboratively and successfully, you will find a group of teachers who are interconnected [and] interdependent" (16). To be successful, collaboration must be driven by teachers, our expertise in our content areas, and our students' needs. Using our flexible model, teachers can collaborate to establish both small and big connections across the disciplines that help students see the connections between what they are learning in their different classes and the connections between that learning and the larger world. What could be more powerful?

REFERENCES

Fisch, Audrey, and Susan Chenelle. 2014. *Using Informational Text to Teach To Kill a Mockingbird*. Lanham, MD: Rowman & Littlefield.

Jones, Stephen. 2010. "The Case for Unpopular Clients." *The Wall Street Journal*, March 13. Accessed March 14, 2013. http://www.wsj.com/articles/SB10001424052748703625304575116250512434096.

Lee, Harper. 2002. Reprint. *To Kill a Mockingbird*. New York: HarperCollins. Original edition, New York: Harper & Row, 1960.

Rami, Meenoo. 2014. *Thrive: 5 Ways to (Re)Invigorate Your Teaching*. Portsmouth, NH: Heinemann.

Acknowledgments

This book came as a result of our work on using informational text to teach literature. We presented our work to teachers in New Jersey, including several times at the New Jersey Association of Supervision and Curriculum Development at Marie Adair's gracious invitation, and across the country at national conferences, and we were struck by the ways in which teachers and administrators were interested in adapting our model for using informational text in order to facilitate collaboration across the disciplines. We were impressed by the many educators eager to rise to the challenge of the informational text mandate of the Common Core and the need for concrete tools to enable literacy connections across the disciplines. This book is our contribution to the ongoing efforts to meet that need so that teachers in all content areas can use informational text to connect: to enhance literacy, motivation, and engagement across the disciplines.

We are grateful to Tom Koerner, Carlie Wall, Anita Singh, and the entire team at Rowman and Littlefield for their ongoing support for our work.

We are also grateful for the institutional support we have had for this project. This includes the invaluable support of Frederick Smith, Laura Kortz, and James Brown at the Guarini Library at New Jersey City University.

Audrey wishes to acknowledge crucial institutional support at New Jersey City University from Allan De Fina, Dean of the Deborah Cannon Partridge Wolfe College of Education; Daniel Julius, Provost; and Sue Henderson, President.

Susan wishes to acknowledge valuable institutional support from Dean Erie Lugo and the Board of Trustees of University Academy Charter High School.

Audrey would also like to acknowledge her wonderful community at New Jersey City University: Debbie Bennett, Erik Morales, Tracy Amerman,

Winifred McNeill, Lourdes Sutton, Alex Kim, Irma Maini, John Bragg, and Vanashri Nargund-Joshi. Thanks also to Max Flysch and Mark Flynn for never-ending support.

Susan would also like to acknowledge her dedicated and inspiring colleagues, particularly Steven Gavrielatos, Edwin Rivera, and Hans Winberg, and her students at University Academy Charter High School, from whom she learns every day. She also wishes to thank Sarah Tantillo for her insight on the important role informational text plays in student literacy. Finally, she would like to thank her partner Ian Cook and her family for their unwavering, essential support.

We would also like to thank Michele Haiken for her enormously thoughtful feedback on our work and Oona Marie Abrams for giving us our first opportunity to write about collaboration in *English Leadership Quarterly*.

Finally, we acknowledge all the teachers across the United States who work every day to make their classrooms a place of substantive inquiry and lively engagement. We hope this book will help you in that enterprise as we all strive to nurture in our students literacy skills for life and an enduring love of learning.

Permissions

The authors and publisher wish to thank those who have generously given permission to reprint material.

Excerpts from "To Study Aggression: A Fight Club for Flies" by James Gorman from *The New York Times*. Copyright © 2014 by *The New York Times*. Reprinted by permission. All rights reserved.

Figure A.1: "To Study Aggression" photograph, copyright © 2014 by Kenta Asahina in The New York Times (February 3, 2014). Used with permission.

Chapter 1

Literacy

Everyone's Responsibility (and Opportunity)

One of the biggest changes brought about by the Common Core State Standards is the creation of cross-content literacy standards.¹

The new literacy standards make literacy instruction a shared responsibility.

For language arts teachers, this innovation is long overdue and very welcome. The language arts teachers no longer shoulder full and sole responsibility for literacy skills.

For content-area teachers, however, there is some trepidation. The science teacher still has the same chemistry content to cover. How is she supposed to make time to teach reading and writing? How, moreover, is she supposed to teach reading and writing when she has not been trained to do so? Her subject is chemistry, not literacy.

Our goal in this volume is to help. We offer a step-by-step approach to literacy instruction through the use of informational texts in a way that enhances rather than takes away from the teaching of content in all our disciplines. We also suggest some methods for collaboration so that this literacy instruction can function as a shared opportunity as well as a shared responsibility.

BUT WHY SHOULD LITERACY BE EVERYONE'S RESPONSIBILITY?

To put it simply, because literacy skills across the content areas are central to success in college and careers. English teacher Meaghan Freeman (2015), writing in *The Atlantic*, puts the need for cross-content literacy well: "Not every child need[s] to be expert at analyzing literature. Every kid in my room is going to read articles on the Internet and use a social studies textbook. Most will farm and read technical manuals for careers. They'll be bombarded with ads, commercials, and campaign speeches that they'll have to analyze and evaluate."

Freeman's students need to be able to read textbooks in college and/or to master the texts of their disparate fields (farm manuals for farmers, technical manuals for those working in technical fields, engineering manuals for engineers, medical journals for doctors, etc.).

All students, moreover, need to be able to manage careful, thoughtful analysis of the variety of complex texts we encounter regularly: "ads, commercials, and campaign speeches," as Freeman notes, and also government documents, court decisions, medical reports, news articles, opinion pieces in all sorts of media, etc. Hopefully, our students will leave high school with some sense of the power of their own voices, so that they can, when they need to, speak and write cogently and convincingly to peers, to bosses, to employees, to political leaders, and in the public sphere generally.

In other words, we want our students to graduate from high school (and even more so from college) ready to master the reading and writing demands of their disciplines, and we also want them to have the skills necessary to express themselves intelligently and successfully as engaged, active citizens in their daily lives.

As the introduction to the Common Core literacy standards states, "Part of the motivation behind the interdisciplinary approach to literacy promulgated by the Standards is extensive research establishing the need for college and career ready students to be proficient in reading complex informational text independently in a variety of content areas" (Common Core State Standards Initiative 2010, 4).

To develop these skills, our students need to be able to operate in a world defined by varied, complex texts, not simply textbooks and novels. Hence, the CCSS mandate that by the time a student reaches the twelfth grade, his or her reading, across all disciplines, should consist of 70 percent informational texts and 30 percent literary texts (2010, 5).

The 70/30 mandate does not mean that 70 percent of the curriculum in any one class must be comprised of informational texts: this is a shared enterprise.

WHAT IS INFORMATIONAL TEXT?

The CCSS aren't particularly clear on this question. Appendix A, "Research Supporting Key Elements of the Standards" (2010), distinguishes between "narrative" and "expository" text and suggests that "expository text makes up the vast majority of the required reading in college and the workplace" and "is harder for most students to read than is narrative text" (3). The CCSS cite research that suggests that students are asked to read too little expository text and that the "little expository reading students are asked to do is too often of the superficial variety that involves skimming and scanning for particular, discrete pieces of information" (3).

Informational text, then, is non-narrative text or expository text.[2] It encompasses the range of nonfiction, both print and nonprint, students and adults encounter every day.

Could content-area teachers of subjects that have been traditionally textbook-based satisfy the letter of the CCSS informational text requirement by having students read the textbook? Not really. And how exciting and engaging do your students generally find your textbook? Not very. Does textbook reading actually prepare young adults for the college, career, and life reading and critical thinking they have ahead of them? No.

In *Real World Literacies: Disciplinary Teaching in the High School Classroom*, Heather Lattimer (2014) articulates the challenge of meeting the literacy needs of our students, a challenge that encompasses but stretches well beyond the Common Core: "We must explicitly nurture habits of mind that will allow students to adapt literacy practices in response to evolving contexts, technologies, and disciplines. The literacy demands that students in our classrooms today will encounter in the workplace, academic sphere, and civic life in five, ten, or twenty years are nearly impossible to foresee" (4).

To meet these literacy demands, we need teaching practices that engage students "in learning experiences that . . . will allow [students] to succeed within disciplines today and prepare them to be successful as they traverse and transfer learning across disciplines and into new fields in the future" (4).

Clearly, then, to satisfy the real spirit and challenge of the CCSS informational text requirement and to provide learning experiences that meet all the literacy needs of our students, content-area teachers, alongside their peers in language arts, need to revisit and rethink the range and kinds of complex informational texts used in the classroom and the ways in which we are using these texts.

LITERACY IN THE DISCIPLINES

After all, few of us read textbooks unless we are preparing to use them in class. But all of us read and work with texts in our disciplines, albeit in different ways.

Scientists read research studies in order to keep up-to-date on the latest experiments and developments in their fields of expertise. Historians read primary documents and new works of historical analysis in order to enhance their own understanding of the past and its bearing on the present. Mathematicians, engineers, and programmers read a variety of texts in their fields in order to stay abreast of the ways their colleagues are using equations, models, and code to understand, predict, and create changes in our physical world.

Even art and music teachers navigate and use words, together with nonverbal modes of meaning and communication, in order to create, order, structure, and understand the world.

The content-area literacy standards, then, as 2010 National Teacher of the Year Sarah Brown Wessling (2012) writes, "empower [our] colleagues in all disciplines to see the power of primary, non-fiction texts [and] remin[d] us that all disciplines are grounded in literacy" (3).

Reading and writing in the disciplines, however, pose particular challenges. Language arts teachers are not well-equipped, on their own, to develop in their students the literacy skills they need in other disciplines (Shanahan and Shanahan 2008). Texts in different disciplines use argument and evidence differently, for example, and place "unique or specialized demands on readers" (ILA 3).

That's why the International Literacy Association insists that it is "imperative that disciplinary literacy instruction be provided by teachers in those fields of study" (ILA 3). So, what does it mean to work with words, to be literate, in science or in music? What are the texts an artistically or scientifically literate person needs to be able to navigate? These are questions teachers in the disciplines are well-equipped to answer. Our aim is to help you incorporate those answers into the classroom in a way that can increase your students' engagement in your content area.

Take for example a project conducted by a math teacher Susan met in her master's degree program. She had her students study the proposed renovations of a major bridge and the nearby port to accommodate new, much larger container ships. The students used their math skills—for example, their understanding of angles, slope, volume, etc.—to analyze and evaluate the impacts of each proposal. They also read news articles, which gave the students an understanding of the concerns of the various stakeholders—for example, the dockworkers who would largely be out of work until the renovation was complete but then would have a lot more work for years to come, the construction workers who would be undertaking the potentially dangerous renovation, and the residents whose daily commute would be severely affected.

In the end, the students used their math skills, their disciplinary literacy, and their understanding of what was at stake in their local environment to fully analyze and evaluate the proposals and then determined which one they thought was the best.

Are there challenges to getting students to read an article in a scientific journal or to make sense out of and write about a piece of statistical analysis? Sure. Proposals about bridge renovations are not easy reading.

But the students in this math class were using all their literacy skills and their content-area knowledge—their math—in a way that made their learning relevant and purposeful. Along the way, they also learned to analyze and critically evaluate the presentation of numeric data and the validity of mathematical claims as arguments (Wilson and Chavez 2014, 95). This is purposeful learning: students tackling the challenging task of making sense out of the world while using both their disciplinary literacy skills and their content knowledge.

So sure, it's challenging, but as Wessling (2012) notes, "Who better to teach students how to maneuver these texts than the teacher-scientists who are with them each day?" (3).

Indeed, who better? Content-area teachers may not be trained to teach reading and writing, but they are the "content area expert[s]" (ILA 5): their fluency in reading and writing in their disciplines makes them more than equipped to teach students "to read like historians, scientists, mathematicians, and literary critics" (ILA 4).

ESSENTIAL QUESTIONS, PURPOSE, AND BIG IDEAS

The issue of purpose is key.

Students need to feel that they are using their disciplinary knowledge to make sense out of the world or about something they care about.

Suppose I am teaching *To Kill a Mockingbird*. What is my purpose? Why am I teaching Harper Lee's novel? What big idea or essential question (Wiggins and McTighe 2014; Burke 2010) do I want my students to take away from the reading?

The answer might be that Lee's novel allows teachers and students across the country to ask not only difficult and enduring but also historically specific and changing questions about race, class, and justice.

That said, language arts teachers don't always consciously ask ourselves the "why *Mockingbird*?" question, and we certainly don't do enough to make our answers explicit to our students.

We need to ask and answer these questions, for ourselves and our students: to make clear why we are studying this text, what it's "about," and why it matters.

Teachers need to answer these sorts of questions in math, history, Spanish, chemistry, and music as well. Why does math matter? Why do we need to understand how the brain works? What purpose is served by studying the War of 1812?

We all have our standards and our curricula, but our more difficult but also more exciting task is to make visible to our students the purpose behind our study each and every day: why are we doing this, why are we learning this, and what's the purpose of it all?

THE OPPORTUNITY OF INFORMATIONAL TEXT

Teacher-selected, timely, relevant informational texts can offer students practice with complex texts, help students discover answers to the essential "why" questions, and transform our classrooms into deeply intellectual places of real learning.

Let's turn to William Golding's *Lord of the Flies* (1955), which is going to serve as our example text throughout this volume. But keep in mind that our discussion and examples can apply to any anchor text or core curriculum topic in any discipline.

Teaching Golding's novel poses a number of challenges. It's about a bunch of British schoolboys. There is literally not one female character. The boys are marooned on a desert island.

Any number of students are likely to ask, in response to this text, "why bother?" or "who cares?" Truth be told, a few teachers might share their students' questions.

A well-chosen informational text can enliven Golding's novel, answering the "why read this" question and motivating students to care about the text and the issues it raises.

One reason to teach *Lord of the Flies* is to think about aggression and bullying, issues central in the lives and schools of many young people today.

Scientists are interested in all sorts of aspects of aggression. Are males more aggressive than females? Are there hormones associated with aggression? Do professional athletes possess higher levels of aggression, and is this aggression responsible for their greater success in competition? Is cruelty the natural and inevitable consequence of a power differential?

All of these topical questions are probably more interesting to your average student than what happens to poor Piggy on that island. Or, to put the matter a different way, all of these questions have the potential to give a purpose to our reading about Piggy.

For this volume, we are going to home in on the issue of male aggression in relation to *Lord of the Flies*. The informational text we've chosen for our pairing is "To Study Aggression: A Fight Club for Flies," written for the *New York Times* by science writer James Gorman (2014). In the piece, Gorman discusses scientific experiments on fruit flies, including genetic modification of flies, the discovery of one gene and a small group of neurons found responsible for aggression, and the conclusion, based on the absence of those neurons in female fruit flies, regarding the relationship between brain chemistry and social behavior in fruit flies.

The connections with Golding's novel are fascinating, and not just because we are talking about flies!

Gorman's article is a rich piece of writing in its own right, worthy of reading for a variety of reasons, including its discussion of scientific process and experimentation, of neuroscience, of how we can and cannot extrapolate from experiments on animals to conclusions about human behavior. Certainly, Gorman's is a high-quality informational text of the kind that we want all our students to be able to read critically, thoughtfully, and with confidence.

And paired with *Lord of the Flies*, the informational text highlights to students why we should care about Piggy and his tormentors and why Golding's novel is perhaps particularly relevant in this time of heightened attention to and examples of adolescent aggression.

The pairing, in other words, helps students to have that aha moment in which they can understand the larger purpose to their reading and work in the classroom.

Surely one of the reasons why the Common Core's ninth anchor standard for reading asks students to "analyze how two or more texts address similar themes or topics in order to build knowledge or to compare the approaches the authors take" (2010, 35) is that context is so crucial for making sense out of any idea.

As teachers, we create the context or framework—for *Lord of the Flies* or for any set of ideas we introduce. When we use another text to create that context, we move the context beyond what students bring to the classroom with their own brains and into a bigger intellectual domain of texts (Wessling 2011, 24) (Textbox 1.1).

Textbox 1.1

Anchor Standard 9 for Reading: Analyze how two or more texts address similar themes or topics in order to build knowledge or to compare the approaches the authors take.

In other words, when teachers select informational texts to use in connection with their curriculum, they take that crucial step back and ask themselves big questions about the framework they want to use to set the conversation in the classroom (Mills and Moon 2014).

What am I trying to teach here? What is the purpose of this lesson? What do my students need to know? And why do they need to know it? What can this knowledge or skill do for students? Why does what I'm teaching matter?

What are the essential questions or big ideas submerged in the lesson and how can I bring those to the surface for the students?

When we ask and answer these questions, our classrooms can come alive for our students (and for ourselves).

INFORMATIONAL TEXT AND THE OPPORTUNITY FOR DIFFERENTIATION

Informational text offers particularly rich opportunities for differentiation in the classroom.

First of all, as we will discuss below, the informational text connection is built by the teacher based on ideas about what might help students connect with or make sense out of the underlying content. That means the teacher is already thinking about the particular needs of his/her group of students, where they are coming from in terms of interests and background knowledge.

Second, as we've talked about above and as we will discuss below, the informational text doesn't need to be a written expository text. Some learners may respond better to video, audio, or graphics. Any of these might be the primary informational text, or, as we will illustrate with the Gorman article, visual and/or audio texts can be used in combination with a written text to make the ideas more accessible to all learners.

Finally, as your students become skilled readers of informational text, you might offer your class an array of print and nonprint texts on which to build connections. Groups of learners might take on and report on different text types, with mixed grouping to provide support.

The range of informational text types multiplies the opportunities for successful differentiation and offers the potential for all the learners in your classroom to develop confidence and mastery over some version of the material.

USING INFORMATIONAL TEXT TO INCREASE MOTIVATION AND ENGAGEMENT

Still, the math teacher queries, how can we find the time and space to include complex informational texts in our classrooms and still help our students master all the material in our content area? How do we teach this new material and still cover all the math?

Think about what we all know about purposeful, effective teaching. When we teach with a clear purpose, our students can grasp the concepts quickly;

when we struggle, our students struggle, and we end up reteaching and using more and more precious time. Articles on how mathematical models are used to predict the progress of epidemics like Ebola or to differentiate between types of tumor cells can help students see what they are learning in class as real and urgent.

When the students can connect to the material and see the purpose of their learning, they can learn efficiently; when they have no idea of the "why" behind what they are being asked to learn, the ideas go in one ear and out the other.

The struggle to teach effectively and efficiently so that we bring all the students along is what makes teaching the interesting profession that it is.

A clearer purpose, through the use of complex informational texts that engage the literacy skills and are meaningful in your discipline, means that your students will be more engaged and efficient learners. The goal is to use informational text to create that motivation and interest.

The Gorman article about aggression in male fruit flies is one example (and not necessarily an example that will work for all students in all classrooms). But the idea behind using this informational text is that it builds literacy skills while offering students a purpose—a reason to care and connect with *Lord of the Flies*. When we create that motivation and engagement, reading Golding's novel becomes a more appealing and rewarding task.

What we offer here is a simple, step-by-step method for finding, preparing, and using informational text in your classroom.

But before we turn to that method, we want to talk about collaboration.

NOTES

1. States working outside the Common Core framework have "adopted their own versions of disciplinary literacy standards" (ILA 2).

2. Oddly, some of the exemplars offered by the Common Core are actually novels, like Richard Wright's *Black Boy*.

REFERENCES

Burke, Jim. 2010. *What's the Big Idea: Question-Driven Units to Motivate Reading, Writing, and Thinking*. Portsmouth, NH: Heinemann.

Common Core State Standards Initiative. 2010a. *Common Core State Standards for English Language Arts and Literacy in History/Social Studies, Science, and Technical Subjects*. Washington, DC.

Common Core State Standards Initiative. 2010b. Appendix A to *Common Core State Standards for English Language Arts and Literacy in History/Social Studies,*

Science, and Technical Subjects. Washington, DC: Common Core State Standards Initiative.

Freeman, Meaghan. 2015. "The Common Core Has Not Killed Literature." *The Atlantic*, February 3. Accessed February 4, 2015. http://www.theatlantic.com/education/archive/2015/02/the-common-core-has-not-killed-literature/385120/.

Golding, William. 2003. Reprint. *Lord of the Flies.* New York: Perigree Books. Original edition, New York: Coward-McCann, Inc., 1955.

Gorman, James. 2014. "To Study Aggression: A Fight Club for Flies." *The New York Times.* February 3. Accessed February 5, 2014. http://www.nytimes.com/2014/02/04/science/to-study-aggression-a-fight-club-for-flies.html.

International Literacy Association (ILA). Common Core State Standards Committee. 2015. *Collaborating for Success: The Vital Role of Content Teachers in Developing Disciplinary Literacy With Students in Grades 6-12.* Newark, DE: International Literacy Association. Accessed June 15, 2015. http://literacyworldwide.org/docs/default-source/where-we-stand/ccss-disciplinary-literacy-statement.pdf?sfvrsn=4.

Lattimer, Heather. 2014. *Real World Literacies: Disciplinary Teaching in the High School Classroom.* Urbana, Ill.: National Council of Teachers of English.

Lee, Harper. 2002. Reprint. *To Kill a Mockingbird.* New York: HarperCollins. Original edition, New York: Harper & Row, 1960.

Mills, Allisyn, and Seungho Moon. 2014. "Teaching Equity through *Gatsby* in the Age of CCSS." *English Journal*, 104.2, 86–92.

Shanahan, Timothy, and Cynthia Shanahan. 2008. "Teaching Disciplinary Literacy to Adolescents: Rethinking Content-Area Literacy." *Harvard Educational Review*, 78.1, 40–59.

Wessling, Sarah. 2011. "Everything's a Conversation: Reading Away Isolation." In *Supporting Students in a Time of Core Standards: English Language Arts, Grades 9–12*, 24–27. Urbana, Ill.: National Council of Teachers of English.

Wessling, Sarah. 2012. "My 10 Greatest "Ah-ha" Moments in Working with the Core." Accessed April 5, 2015. https://dqam6mam97sh3.cloudfront.net/resources/uploaded_document/resource/11/CCSS_whitepaper.pdf.

Wiggins, Grant, and Jay McTighe 2014. *Understanding by Design: Guide to Creating High-Quality Units.* Alexandria, Va.: ASCD.

Wilson, Amy Alexandra, and Kathryn J. Chavez. 2014. *Reading and Representing Across the Content Areas: A Classroom Guide.* New York: Teachers College Press.

Chapter 2

Collaboration

The Gift of the Common Core

Long before the advent of the Common Core, teachers were collaborating to find ways to get their students to read and write across the disciplines.

But surely one central gift of the Core is the emphasis on collaboration. After all, speaking and listening anchor standard 1 asks students to "prepare for and participate effectively in a range of conversations and collaborations with diverse partners, building on others' ideas and expressing their own clearly and persuasively" (2010, 48) (Textbox 2.1).

Textbox 2.1

> **Anchor Standard 1 for Speaking and Listening:** Prepare for and participate effectively in a range of conversations and collaborations with diverse partners, building on others' ideas and expressing their own clearly and persuasively.

What better way to inspire students in this enterprise than for teachers to have these conversations themselves: preparing for and collaborating on learning experiences with diverse teaching partners and building on other teachers' ideas.

Moreover, as the International Literacy Association reminds us, "When ELA teachers collaborate with content teachers, students better understand how to read and write informational text well . . . . [At the same time] both ELA standards and content area standards are more likely to be met and students will develop a deeper understanding of the content" (ILA 5).

This is part of the idea behind our fruit flies and *Lord of the Flies* pairing. If the science teacher and the language arts teacher collaborate in creating a lesson around the Gorman article on fruit fly experiments, the students' literacy skills will be enhanced but so too will their cross-disciplinary skills.

Regardless of whether both teachers actually teach the informational text in their classes or whether only one teacher devotes class time to the text, both teachers can reference the content, drawing on and using the ideas of the text. The disciplinary content—of the scientific process, for example, and of *Lord of the Flies*—is enhanced by the cross-disciplinary exercise.

And all this can be done through collaboration over one small informational text.

After all, we need to acknowledge that teaching is busy, labor-intensive work, and we all struggle to find enough hours in the day to do all we want to do with our curriculum and our students. We aren't suggesting you rethink your entire curriculum and spend weeks drafting a new one based on a utopian shared set of texts and ideas.

We live in the real world.

Let's not underestimate the power of small collaborations, however.

Collaboration, after all, can help us make the most of the time and effort we devote to our instruction. To be successful, however, collaboration, big or small, must be driven by teachers and our expertise in our content areas and our students' needs.

OPTIMISM

There's cause for optimism. In "The 'Amazing Things' Teachers Can Do Together," Philip Johnson (2015) writes about educators in Downers Grove, Illinois, who have been working to create integrated learning targets and common assessment rubrics across the disciplines and in alignment with the Common Core.[1]

The group included 30 teachers and numerous department heads from nearly every department in the school. A cynic might think a project of this size and diversity could only end in disaster: two teachers, three opinions; 30 teachers, chaos.

What's striking about this project, however, was the "immediate buy-in" (2015, 13) as described by department chairperson and now associate principal of curriculum and instruction, Janice Schwarze. Teacher Chris Esposito suggests that this vital buy-in arose out of a basic and fairly easily achieved consensus over the ideas of the Core: "Every citizen needs to be able to be skilled at discussion, to be able to communicate ideas, to critically listen to what is going on in the world around her. . . . Within that critical framework, it was easy for a lot of teachers to say this is an important kind of education" (2015, 13).

The group of educators could get past "illusory barriers between disciplines" and instead attend to the task of "refocusing students' minds on universally applicable thinking skills" (2015, 13).

What's important about the work of teachers at Downers Grove is the potential it illustrates for educators, when we recognize how we share goals, to put our many hands and minds together to do great things.

Our approach to incorporating informational texts, as we'll outline in this volume, offers a way to demystify the process so that teachers can feel confident in finding, preparing, and teaching informational text units—both for their own classrooms and in collaboration with colleagues—in an organic way that connects with their curriculum and their students. In this volume, we'll offer step-by-step examples and instructions for building cross-disciplinary connections around complex, engaging informational texts.

TIME, SCHEDULES, CHAOS

In theory, cross-disciplinary collaboration is organic, clean, and tidy.

Take, for example, the story of two eighth-grade teachers in science and language arts, from Adel DeSoto Minburn Community School District in Adel, Iowa. We attended the impressive session at ASCD 2015, "Collaboration that Works: Science, Literacy, and 21st Century Skills," in which Kate Cronk and Hallie Edgerly presented their story of spectacular collaboration across the disciplines.

They spoke about their three-year process (totally self-initiated and self-motivated) of developing a four-week cross-disciplinary unit on inventions. Their students read about and conducted market research, including firsthand surveys, developed budgets and marketing materials, kept logs of their invention timelines, and reflected on their collaborative skills. They used QR codes to link to student-created infomercials about their products. The unit culminated in a visit to a local college and a *Shark Tank*-style competition. There is no question that Cronk and Edgerly's students were developing and using twenty-first-century skills.

Equally impressive, from the many student testimonials they shared, was the pride these two young teachers took in how their collaborative, cross-disciplinary project fostered their students' social and academic skills, brought out the strengths of individual students with specific weaknesses, and even reduced absenteeism and bullying.

Cronk and Edgerly were frank about their own learning process: how they needed to improve on their own interactions with other teachers, how they involved other teachers even when those teachers were unable to give up classroom time, and how they both grew as teachers from the project.

What's perhaps most impressive in Cronk and Edgerly's work is how it was simply the age-old tale of two individuals with initiative putting in the work and making a tremendous difference in the lives of the children in their school.

But let's also be clear about some of the tremendous advantages these two teachers had. They shared one set of students and a prep period for planning. They were able to align their curricula, map a collaborative unit, visit each other's classes, and co-teach certain aspects of the unit. Over time, they were able to cultivate and develop administrative support and resources outside their classrooms.

Yes, they are two energetic teachers with initiative and creativity, but there is no one model for successful collaboration, and high school teachers do not need to envision a fully integrated four-week unit when thinking about cross-disciplinary collaboration.

Don't be put off by the examples of polished and fully functional collaborations you may read about or see around you. Be inspired by those and remember they involved years of work, many mistakes, and lots of false starts.

As social studies teacher Lauren Francese and English teacher Rebecca Marsick note in *Stretching Beyond the Textbook*, in the beginning of their collaborative relationship, they simply coordinated curricula; for example, Marsick would teach *To Kill a Mockingbird*, while Francese discussed Jim Crow (2014, 97). Eventually, they started to collaborate more fully by organizing their *Mockingbird*-Civil Rights unit around common essential questions, like "What does it mean to be a strong leader?" and "Can young people make a difference?" They would then ask their students to consider these questions in terms of both *Mockingbird* in English and *Claudette Colvin: Twice Toward Justice* in social studies (105).

The key is to seek out what's possible now, do that, and then build on it.

Even one day of connection is valuable. Start small. Allow yourself room for failure. Remember that collaboration is messy.

Cronk and Edgerly discussed the ways in which their collaborative work and their process was off-putting and threatening to some of their colleagues (and shared how they adjusted to address this issue). Of course, the more common problem is the interactions between the primary collaborative partners. Who takes the initiative? Who watches over the details? How are power disparities (of age, of experience, of discipline) negotiated?

Collaboration, moreover, isn't a finite activity. These units can't be one-size-fits-all or set-it-and-forget-it. When using informational texts in our own classrooms, we can't pick a great article and assume that it and the lesson(s) we build around it will work year after year. An informational text connection that may work well in one time at one school with one set of students may not work well in another setting or with another set of students at another moment in time. Collaboration must grow and evolve to suit the changing needs and capacities of your students—and those of your colleagues and/or school as a whole.

The only collaboration that is totally doomed to fail is the one you are afraid to start. And collaborating with a colleague on teaching an informational text relevant to both of your respective content areas is a practical and rewarding place to start.

START WITH SOMEONE YOU LIKE

Cronk and Edgerly did not begin their collaboration because an administrator told them to do so. They did not share a common teaching philosophy or vision of the curriculum. They began to work together because, as they shared with the audience at ASCD, they both were young, new teachers—with time (no families) and without many friends or allies at their school (new teachers!). They were green: nervous, ready to work, looking for peers.

These relatively mundane (and relatively common) qualities, rather than some shared, theoretically sophisticated view of education, brought the two together.

Along the way, Cronk and Edgerly learned about their shared but also differing educational approaches; they also learned about give-and-take and compromise.

In Susan's school, sophomore English teacher Steven Gavrielatos and geometry teacher Edwin Rivera collaborated to create an innovative project that helped students see the connections between concepts, like syllogism, reciprocity, and parallelism, that are used in both disciplines.

Students completed exercises in each class in which they applied their understanding of each concept. For example, in English class, they worked with sample sentences to draw syllogistic inferences, breaking them down into key components of logical argumentation: premise and conclusion. Then, in geometry, they used the law of syllogism to draw logical conclusions from statements about geometric shapes. Finally, they synthesized new examples of each.

After completing the exercises, students reflected in writing on the similarities and differences between how a concept they had studied is used in English and how the same concept is used in geometry and then also demonstrated their comparison using a Venn diagram.

The students were so excited to see the relevance of the knowledge they had acquired in one class validated in another that Susan's own sophomores demanded to take part in the cross-disciplinary project as well. Susan was of course happy to oblige and loved getting to see her students take ownership of their learning in this way and gain confidence in the value of their knowledge and their ability to apply it.

And all of this rich, wonderful learning came out of the friendship between the teachers who initiated it.

Again, a math teacher and an English teacher, who happened to get along, were able to come together to design a deeply intellectual, cross-disciplinary collaboration. It's worth remembering that the potential for collaboration exists across all the disciplines—not just the obvious ones like social studies and language arts.

Steer away, at least initially until you build your collaborative chops, from departments or people whose interests and egos threaten to get in the way. That friendly new faculty member from the music department, with whom you've had amiable conversation at lunch or at a school event, may be a terrific person with whom to start a conversation, even if you are a science teacher.

Think outside the box and reach out to a person with whom you think you'd like to spend time!

SHARE INFORMATION AND ASK FOR EXPERT HELP

The key to collaboration is sharing information: about your content, about your students' needs and interests, about your instructional goals. Whether you're working with a single, like-minded colleague or trying to foster collaboration school-wide, start by initiating and facilitating communication.

One way to think about these conversations is to understand the wealth of knowledge present and often underutilized at every school. As teachers, all of us come face to face with the challenge of teaching a difficult text, topic, or idea that is slightly outside of our area of expertise. Perhaps we shy away from this teaching challenge because it seems too hard or we don't have the time to bone up on the new material. But we are forgetting that we have experts in these fields just down the hall, and they are not only experts in these disciplines but they also know our students.

When Susan was studying *The Great Gatsby* with her sophomore English class this past year, she wanted her students to read an excerpt of a U.S. Supreme Court decision on prohibition in order to understand some of the novel's context. After excerpting the text and preparing guided reading questions for her lesson, she realized that it would likely be fruitful to run her materials and lesson plan by her students' history teachers, so she sent them the materials and the lesson plan via email.

This action led to a brief but enormously helpful conversation with one of the history teachers later that day. He outlined the way he teaches Supreme Court decisions and the language he uses to frame students' analysis of what is at stake in a decision. He reminded Susan that students need to understand that a Supreme Court case is different from more common kinds of court cases in the respect that no one is being found innocent or guilty, but instead the constitutionality of a law or action is being determined.

This five-minute conversation helped Susan not only focus and feel more confident in her own instruction about the prohibition court case but also gave her the opportunity to draw upon and reinforce her students' existing knowledge about Supreme Court cases, which in turn made her students feel more confident in tackling the challenging excerpt of the decision.

While a one-time email can provide significant dividends, providing a venue to facilitate communication on an ongoing basis can really help collaboration take off. Using a social media platform like Google Drive can make information sharing easy.

Susan created a spreadsheet in Google Drive that teachers use to list the key topics, vocabulary, and texts they will be teaching in upcoming months.[2] Making this information available has helped teachers identify moments when they can draw on students' knowledge from another class, reinforce key vocabulary from class to class, or even change up the order in which teachers teach certain texts or topics in order to align better with what students are doing in another class.

As highlighted in the English-math collaboration described above, making these kinds of connections can be enormously rewarding. Students get to see the connections between the disciplines and their classes. They enter one class already feeling smart because of what they know in another. They build confidence in transferring their knowledge and their analytical skills from one room and setting to another. Eventually this translates into the ability to make connections beyond the classroom, so that students can begin to develop real understanding of the forces that shape their world.

But, again, remember that it's OK to start small. Make collaboration a priority in your mind and opportunities to do so will appear. Think about how your own curriculum materials might intersect with other content areas and remember that even just a simple email asking for help or a brief conversation can foster valuable continuity in teaching strategies in ways that tap into and reinforce students' knowledge from one class and make them feel smart in another. And that kind of rewarding spark will likely lead to more.

TIME FOR COLLABORATION

It goes without saying that teachers never have enough time to talk with one another. We may have classrooms next to each other, but that doesn't mean we have time for conversation at all, let alone the kind of substantive and sustained conversation necessary for collaboration.

So, focus your attention on two areas.

First, ask your administrators for common grade-level planning time.

Second, ask your administrators for professional development time during which teachers can work collaboratively. Even better, offer to lead a professional development workshop focused on collaboration.

A 2014 survey conducted by the National Center on Literacy Education (Nelson 2014) bolsters these demands. According to the survey findings, successful collaboration requires:

- the practice of bringing educators "in all the disciplines together" to address the instructional changes necessary to address "shifting literacy practices"
- the creation of "teacher ownership" by "providing space and support for [teachers] to innovate and design the lessons and materials that are right for their students"

Ask the teachers to identify in advance (or come prepared to identify at the workshop) two or three units that they feel uninspired about, that they feel the students struggle with, or that they think might make work well for some sort of collaboration. At the same time, ask the teachers to let you know about someone with whom they might like to collaborate. Then, make some teams and let the work begin.

This kind of work won't immediately lead to grand, sustainable projects for every team. But it will get the ball rolling. And once one team begins to succeed, ask that team to present their collaboration, however small, to the larger group. Use their success to build momentum. Celebrate the small successes to create a climate for continued work.

NOTES

1. It's worth noting here that the National Center for Literacy Education's online Literacy in Learning Exchange is an important resource that facilitates collaboration among educators in Downers Grove and elsewhere. In addition to providing a venue for sharing ideas about collaboration and literacy, the Exchange offers an Asset Inventory that emerging and established teams can complete and send back to NCLE for analysis and suggestions for next steps on initiating or jump-starting collaboration in their school or district.

2. See www.usinginformationaltext.org/collaboration to access the template for the Google Drive spreadsheet Susan and her colleagues use. However, other social media tools, like Schoology or even an internal blog or wiki, can work just as well, especially if it's a platform that teachers already feel comfortable using.

REFERENCES

Common Core State Standards Initiative. 2010. *Common Core State Standards for English Language Arts and Literacy in History/Social Studies, Science, and Technical Subjects.* Washington, DC.

Cronk, Kate, and Hallie Edgerly. 2015. "Collaboration that Works: Science, Literacy, and 21st Century Skills." Lecture presented at the annual conference for ASCD, Houston, Texas: March 21–23.

Francese, Lauren K., and Rebecca H. Marsick. 2014. *Stretching Beyond the Textbook: Reading and Succeeding With Complex Texts in the Content Areas.* New York: Scholastic.

International Literacy Association (ILA). Common Core State Standards Committee. 2015. *Collaborating for Success: The Vital Role of Content Teachers in Developing Disciplinary Literacy With Students in Grades 6–12.* Newark, DE: International Literacy Association. Accessed June 15, 2015. http://literacyworldwide.org/docs/default-source/where-we-stand/ccss-disciplinary-literacy-statement.pdf?sfvrsn=4.

Johnson, Philip. 2015. "The 'Amazing Things' Teachers Can Do Together." *The Council Chronicle,* March, 11–13.

Nelson, Catherine. 2014. "Teacher Collaboration: Keys to Common Core Success." *Literacy in Learning Exchange,* March 13. http://www.literacyinlearningexchange.org/blog/teacher-collaboration-keys-common-core-success.

Chapter 3

Our Model for Finding and Using Great Informational Texts

A MODEL THAT WORKS FOR EVERYONE

Even though we now have you convinced of the potential rewards of incorporating informational text into your curriculum and the even greater rewards of doing so in collaboration with one or more colleagues, actually doing so may still seem a little daunting. So, in this section, we'll outline our model for how and when to do so. Based on our work with teachers in all disciplines, we offer this model as one that teachers in all content areas will find productive and manageable.

If you are an English teacher, working alone or with a cross-disciplinary colleague, this model will help you use informational text to build engagement with the anchor texts (whether literary or informational) in your curriculum.

If you are a content-area teacher, working alone or in collaboration with an English teacher or another content-area teacher, this model will give you practical support in developing your students' literacy and engagement in your discipline.

If you are collaborating with one or more colleagues, this model will help you support each other in building your students' engagement and literacy in your respective disciplines and critical thinking about the connections between them.

YOU CAN DO THIS

As we discussed earlier, the Common Core makes literacy everyone's responsibility—and that's a good thing. If this new reality makes you nervous, it's important to keep in mind a few things:

1. Each of us is an expert in what it means to be literate in our discipline: expert in reading and interpreting the types of texts that are essential to our discipline.
2. English teachers are not experts in what it means to be literate in other disciplines, and they will need help when teaching a text related to another discipline. The Common Core's literacy standards for grades 6–12 are divided into two parts: ELA and history/social studies and technical subjects. "This division reflects the unique, time-honored place of ELA teachers in developing students' literacy skills while at the same time recognizing that teachers in other areas must have a role in this development as well" (2010, 4). In other words, no matter how much, how widely, or how well students read in their English classes, those skills won't necessarily translate into proficiency in reading and interpreting scientific studies as a scientist or primary historical documents as a historian.
3. We're here to help. This is challenging work, but this model will help you make the most of your time and efforts.

WHEN TO USE INFORMATIONAL TEXT

But, before we get to the how, let's take a moment to think about the when. When do students struggle and why? Informational text can help when:

- you and/or your students are having trouble engaging with the content
- you want your students to have greater background knowledge or context (but you don't want to lecture)
- you want your students to be better readers and thinkers (and that's always, right?)

Think of one unit in your existing curriculum that students struggle with, one that you know is critically important but that tends to not go as well as you would like. As you read through this section, keep that unit in mind and let yourself start to envision how you might use our model to reinvigorate your instruction.

HOW TO FIND GREAT INFORMATIONAL TEXTS

Once you've identified a place in your curriculum where you want to incorporate an informational text to serve one or more of the needs listed above, the next task is to find a text that will accomplish that goal.

Think about the background knowledge students need to fully access the importance of your key text or topic. Resist the inclination to open a textbook and hope it has an easily digestible, one-page background summary to use. Think about real texts that will help your students discover the relevance and significance of the topic.

Is there a news report or editorial about the issue or events you're studying written during that time period? Is there a transcript of an interview with someone who lived at that time? Is there an excerpt of a primary source that can make it seem more real and relevant to your students?

When researching our volume *Using Informational Text to Teach A Raisin in the Sun* (2016), we found a fascinating 1955 report by the City of Chicago Commission on Human Relations detailing daily violent incidents surrounding the desegregation of a public housing project. (This was a difficult piece to find and secure, but more discussion on the sometimes simple process of locating interesting reading pieces is offered below.)

Susan used this material when teaching *A Raisin in the Sun* to her sophomores this year, and they said reading the excerpt from the report, an informational text, helped them understand more clearly that what Lorraine Hansberry depicted in her play wasn't something she made up but something real people actually experienced.

Think about how that key text or topic you are teaching is evident in and/or relevant to an issue or situation going on in the world, preferably something that your students are already concerned about or interested in, or likely would be if they read an engaging text about it. There are likely numerous articles—ranging from general interest to academic—written about that issue or situation that could help students see your content at work in their world.

Let's take our example of *Lord of the Flies*. We identified the novel as potentially remote, uninteresting, and inaccessible to students. We then identified a contemporary issue—aggression, particularly male aggression—that is relevant to students today. And we had a friend in the science department who was amenable to collaboration.

Our task then was to find a contemporary text on the topic of aggression with a scientific slant. A quick Google search with the key words "aggression" and "The New York Times" produced exactly what we were looking for—including a fun video clip to go with it (more on the importance of using multimedia later).

Sometimes you'll find the right piece with your first Internet search; other times it can be a very time-consuming hunt.

KEY TIPS AND SOURCES

We have listed below several tried-and-true sources for engaging informational texts in a variety of disciplines (Table 3.1). But first, here are four key tips for getting off to a strong start:

- *Get to know the New York Times Learning Network.* Written and edited by teachers, the New York Times Learning Network is an enormous trove of lesson plans based on timely articles related to all content areas as well as commonly taught novels. Browsing through its resources is an effective way to jump-start your search in terms of finding great texts but also of seeing the different kinds of connections you could make. The Learning Network's "Text to Text" series is an especially valuable resource for English teachers who are looking for connections to spark student interest in the literary works in their curriculum and that might spark collaboration with a content-area colleague as well. Our lesson plan for *Lord of the Flies* (2015), published on the Learning Network website, contains discussion questions that put a key excerpt from *Lord of the Flies* into dialogue with Gorman's article, embedded video clips about the fruit fly study and of the 1963 movie trailer, and links to other informational texts that students and teachers can use to explore related topics like aggression in girls and athletes, cyberbullying, the Stanford Prison Experiment, and adolescent violence.
- *Set Google news alerts for topic-related key words.* One of the challenges of incorporating informational text into your curriculum is finding the right text when you need it. Let Google's news alerts do some of this work for you. Go to www.google.com/alerts and follow the prompts to set up alerts for various key words related to topics or texts you'll be teaching in the coming weeks or months. Google will then send you an email listing the articles it has found, according to the frequency that you select. You can customize the alert to look for only certain types of sources, from a certain region, and in a particular language. Setting up a weekly alert for "American Dream" during the summer helped Susan find several timely texts that enlivened her teaching of *The Great Gatsby* in the fall.
- *Ask your school librarian (if you are fortunate enough to have one) for ideas.* Your librarian likely knows the ins and outs of the research databases your school has access to, so he or she can be an enormously valuable resource, especially in terms of finding great primary sources that you might not otherwise think to look for.
- *And of course, ask your content-area colleagues about what publications they read to stay up-to-date in their discipline and/or use in their classes.* They may be able to point you to relatively student-friendly resources or articles in their disciplines.

As you start looking for informational texts and considering possible candidates to incorporate, other questions will likely arise. A relevant text might seem too long or its language and vocabulary too complex; its structure might deviate from the key point you want to use it to address. Fear not; we will discuss how to address these concerns in the next chapter/section.

RESOURCES

Here are some quality resources (E=elementary, M=middle school, H=high school) that can cut down your search time. News outlets like *The New York Times*, *CNN*, or *The Wall Street Journal* are of course also worth looking at; we've focused our list here on those you might not find or think of so readily (Table 3.1). (Visit usinginformationaltext.org for updated URLs and resources.)

Again, remember, don't dismiss an otherwise engaging informational text because it seems too long or too difficult. Finding that article, editorial, or study that will help your students discover the relevance and import of your

Table 3.1 Resources

CURRENT EVENTS / ISSUES	
NYT Learning Network (M, H)	http://learning.blogs.nytimes.com/
The NYT LN offers lesson plans for all disciplines related to current events and issues, using present and past *New York Times* articles, videos, and more. Access to articles linked from lesson plans is free and not limited to the nytimes.com paywall.	
Newsela (E, M, H)	http://www.newsela.com/
Newsela offers recent articles from partner media outlets (e.g., Associated Press and The Washington Post) in five versions aimed at a range of Lexile levels, along with quizzes and discussion questions. Newsela PRO allows students to annotate the articles.	
PBS NewsHour Extra (M, H)	http://www.pbs.org/newshour/extra/
PBS News Hour Extra offers multimedia lesson plans on current events for grades 7–12.	
Vox (M, H)	http://vox.com/
Vox publishes engaging, accessible articles that not only report on current events and issues in the news but also explain the concepts involved in them.	
TweenTribune (M, H)	http://tweentribune.com/
Hosted by the Smithsonian, TweenTribune offers recent news stories, photos, graphics, and audio and video materials on current events, history, art, culture, and science for grades K–12, with versions of articles for different Lexile levels—and in Spanish as well.	
CNN Student News (M, H)	http://www.cnn.com/studentnews/
CNN Student News posts daily video news reports produced for middle and high school audiences.	
Time for Kids (M)	http://www.timeforkids.com/
Time for Kids offers current events articles, videos, and activities for middle school students.	
Slate (H)	http://www.slate.com
Slate offers current events articles and thought-provoking opinion pieces, which often assume a high level of background knowledge.	
DOGOnews (E, M)	http://www.dogonews.com
DOGOnews publishes original articles on current events, sports, books, and movies for kids.	

Continued

Table 3.1 Continued

CURRENT EVENTS / ISSUES	
Kelly Gallagher's Article of the Week (H)	http://kellygallagher.org/article-of-the-week

Gallagher posts links to the articles and lesson plans he uses in his high school classes each week. His site also hosts an archive of articles from past years.

The Digital Textbook (H)	http://englishcompanion.com/resources/digital-textbook/

Jim Burke's Digital Textbook offers a collection of resources for teaching students how to read and write from a wide variety of texts.

CoreStand (E, M, H)	http://www.corestand.com/lessons-and-more/

CoreStand offers a weekly newsletter for elementary, middle, and high school teachers, highlighting news stories of the week, along with related English, social studies, and math lesson plans and materials.

HISTORY, SCIENCE, ECONOMICS, TECHNOLOGY, and HEALTH	
Library of Congress (M, H)	http://www.loc.gov/teachers/

The Library of Congress offers a vast wealth of primary source documents and teacher-created lesson plans.

National Archives (M, H)	http://www.docsteach.org

The National Archives also offers a trove of primary source documents and related activities.

EDSITEment! (E, M, H)	http://edsitement.neh.gov/lesson-plans

The National Endowment for the Humanities offers lesson plans featuring a wide variety of sources on art and culture, world languages, history and social studies, and literature.

Facing History and Ourselves (M, H)	http://www.facinghistory.org

Facing History and Ourselves offers a wealth of resources to help teachers create thoughtful inquiry and dialogue about events and issues like the Holocaust, racism, slavery, etc.

ThinkCERCA (M, H)	http://www.thinkcerca.com

ThinkCERCA offers a large library of informational and literary texts and question sets for grades 4–12 on a wide range of topics; teachers can also upload their own texts to create their own lessons.

CommonLit (M, H)	http://www.commonlit.org

CommonLit is an innovative project started by teachers that offers informational and literary texts on a wide variety of common themes, organized by grade and reading level.

TeachingAmericanHistory.org (M, H)	http://www.teachingamericanhistory.org

A project of the Ashbrook Center at Ashland University, this website offers 50 core historical documents, as well as professional development resources for teachers.

Delancey Place (H)	http://www.delanceyplace.com

This blog posts excerpts from an eclectic range of noteworthy nonfiction books on a daily basis.

Psychology Today (M, H)	http://www.psychologytoday.com/

Psychology Today is a reliable source for engaging articles of manageable length and reading level on a wide variety of topics.

Table 3.1 Continued

HISTORY, SCIENCE, ECONOMICS, TECHNOLOGY, and HEALTH	
ReadWorks (M, H)	http://www.readworks.org

ReadWorks offers articles, activities, and lesson plans on a wide variety of topics, many featuring paired texts.

Scientific American (M, H)	http://www.scientificamerican.com

Scientific American offers articles and features of varying length and depth on a wide range of timely scientific topics and trends.

ScienceDaily (M, H)	http://www.sciencedaily.com/

ScienceDaily is a great resource for brief news articles on the latest science discoveries and research.

Phys.org (M, H)	http://www.phys.org

Phys.org offers accessible articles on current developments in physics, nanotechnology, chemistry, astronomy, biology, and other fields.

Teens and Their Money (M, H)	http://www.fool.com/teens/teens01.htm

The Motley Fool offers a series of entertaining articles for teens on various issues related to personal finance and investing.

Business Week (M, H)	http://www.businessweek.com

Business Week offers accessible articles on the economy, finance, and industry.

Forbes (H)	http://www.forbes.com

Forbes publishes a wide range of accessible articles on the economy, finance, and industry, as well as tips for success in business and professional life.

TeensHealth (M, H)	http://teenshealth.org/teen/

TeensHealth offers student-friendly articles on health issues that affect them.

Who's Counting (H)	http://abcnews.go.com/Technology/WhosCounting/

Who's Counting is a series of articles from the early 2000s in which math professor John Allen Paulos analyzed then-current events from a mathematician's point of view.

Wired (H)	http://www.wired.com

Wired offers articles of varying length and depth on all things related to technology.

Wonderopolis (M)	http://www.wonderopolis.com

Wonderopolis offers informational resources focused on a "wonder of the day," which can be related to a wide range of topics.

SPORTS and ENTERTAINMENT—Articles on sports and entertainment can also be found on the general interest/current events resources listed above.	
NPR music/entertainment (M, H)	http://www.npr.org/series/100920965/music-articles/

National Public Radio's archive of music and entertainment-related stories offers both text and audio resources on popular and emerging artists.

Sports Illustrated for Kids (M, H)	http://www.sikids.com

Sports Illustrated for Kids offers sports news articles and interactive features aimed at middle and high school students.

content is only the first step. In the following chapters, we'll talk about how to set your students up for success with an informational text by addressing any challenges in terms of length, structure, and vocabulary.

REFERENCES

City of Chicago. 1955. Chicago Commission on Human Relations. *The Trumbull Park Homes Disturbances: A Chronological Report*. Chicago.

Common Core State Standards Initiative. 2010. *Common Core State Standards for English Language Arts and Literacy in History/Social Studies, Science, and Technical Subjects*. Washington, DC.

Fisch, Audrey, and Susan Chenelle. 2016. *Using Informational Text to Teach A Raisin in the Sun*. Lanham, Md.: Rowman & Littlefield.

Fisch, Audrey, and Susan Chenelle. 2015. "Text to Text: 'Lord of the Flies' and 'A Fight Club for Flies.'" *The New York Times Learning Network*, January 22. http://learning.blogs.nytimes.com/2015/01/22/text-to-text-lord-of-the-flies-and-a-fight-club-for-flies/.

Golding, William. 2003. Reprint. *Lord of the Flies*. New York: Perigree Books. Original edition, New York: Coward-McCann, Inc., 1955.

Gorman, James. 2014. "To Study Aggression: A Fight Club for Flies." *The New York Times*, February 3. http://www.nytimes.com/2014/02/04/science/to-study-aggression-a-fight-club-for-flies.html.

Hansberry, Lorraine. 1994. *A Raisin in the Sun*. New York: Vintage.

Chapter 4

Preparing an Informational Text

Finding a great informational text is just the first step. Like many kinds of complex texts, informational texts often come with hurdles that challenge both students and teachers. The key is to set ourselves up for success by anticipating stumbling blocks and sufficiently scaffolding the reading process.

Students may not be prepared to read a particular informational text for a variety of reasons: overall length, challenging or unfamiliar structure, complex writing style, distracting or irrelevant ideas, and/or unfamiliar vocabulary. In this section, we'll address length.

DON'T OVERLOAD YOUR STUDENTS

While we want to expose our students to rigorous texts, that doesn't mean that they always have to read the entire text every single time. When challenging our students to read a lengthy, complete text and to focus on it for an extended length of time is central to our instructional goals, then we should do so. But it often isn't. We do not want to shy away from readings of challenging length, but many informational texts are too long for the time we can devote to them in class and/or go beyond our instructional goals.

So, use excerpts. Cut out what you don't need. Really, you can. It's OK; we promise.

Once you've chosen your informational text, read through it carefully to determine which parts of it are essential to your instructional goals and which are not and might even distract from your goals. Try to keep essential features of the text intact, but exclude material that does not serve your instructional purposes.

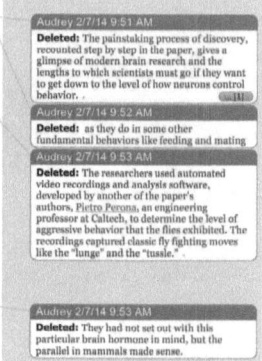

The research began, Dr. Anderson said, with the hypothesis that neuropeptides, which are a kind of hormone in the brain, had a role in controlling aggression.

To find out which neuropeptides were important, the team tested different lines, of genetically modified fruit flies. All lines had been engineered so that at a certain temperature, around 80 degrees, a chemical change would make specific neurons fire. In each line the neurons were different. They tested about 40 lines of flies, raising the temperature to increase the firing of neurons and determine which flies showed increased aggressive behavior. They used another technique to make neurons they were studying become fluorescent green so they could see their anatomy and location. And using a variety of tools, they narrowed the search to neurons that were producing the neuropeptide tachykinin. When they compared the brains of male and female flies, they found a few neurons, present only in the male, that produced tachykinin. When these neurons were silenced, the researchers were able to decrease aggression. The emergence of tachykinin was very interesting because mammals have several different kinds of tachykinin, including substance P, which has been connected to aggression in rodents and has a variety of suspected roles in human beings, including a possible link to aggression.

They now had identified a cluster of neurons, as few as three, that caused an increase in aggression. Those few neurons were only in males. They were active when males were fighting each other. The researchers did more genetic manipulation, deleting and adding

Figure 4.1 Note here how extensively we cut the article. Don't be afraid to remove anything that distracts from your instructional goals.

For example, when we began working with the *New York Times* article on the study of aggression in male fruit flies, we decided that we wanted our excerpt to focus strictly on the findings of the study and what they suggest about aggression in humans.

In the end, as Figure 4.1 illustrates, we cut the article down substantially, from 1,043 to 688 words, removing details about the study's methodology, how the scientists recorded the flies' behavior, and the context the article provides about the state of modern brain research.

At 1,043 words, originally, the article wasn't overly long, but it contained a significant amount of information that was not essential to our instructional goals in relation to *Lord of the Flies* and would have simply slowed our lesson down and undermined the focus of our instruction.

We took out, for example, the detail about how jilted male fruit flies turned to drink because, amusing as it was, it was irrelevant to the issue of aggression and certainly could have proved distracting. Removing these sections did not impair students' comprehension of key ideas or their ability to make meaningful connections with *Lord of the Flies*.

BUT LISTEN TO YOUR COLLABORATION PARTNER

If you are using an informational text in collaboration with a partner from another content area, then it is critically important that you undertake this step together. What might be nonessential to your instructional goals might be absolutely critical to those of your partner.

For example, a science teacher might be interested in the role of automated video recordings and analysis software in the scientific experimentation in our fruit fly article. Work together to strike a balance between your respective needs and what your students are ready for—both in terms of learning content and developing their general and discipline-specific literacy skills. You should end up with an excerpt that works for both of you, rather than different versions, which could end up confusing students.

The keys are to clearly identify your instructional goals, use them to make the excerpt manageable in terms of length, and cut out potentially distracting and irrelevant sections. Doing these steps successfully will allow you to make the most of the text without eating up lots of precious class time.

REFERENCE

Gorman, James. 2014. "To Study Aggression: A Fight Club for Flies." *The New York Times*, February 3. http://www.nytimes.com/2014/02/04/science/to-study-aggression-a-fight-club-for-flies.html.

Chapter 5

Making Vocabulary Work

Vocabulary is often one of the challenges posed by informational texts. A newspaper article or editorial, let alone a scientific study or mathematical analysis, can be full of words and phrases unfamiliar to our students.

But, before you get too discouraged, keep in mind three things: (1) many of these words are words our students should know and need to learn, (2) using new words in a meaningful, purposeful context is the best way to learn them, and (3) you can use the vocabulary work you do to support student success and engagement with the content of the informational text overall.

As Fisher and Frey (2015) put it, "Rigorous, engaging vocabulary instruction . . . give[s] students many opportunities to interact with vocabulary in meaningful ways" (77).

So, let's talk about how to turn vocabulary from a daunting challenge into a meaningful, rewarding opportunity.

IDENTIFY KEY VOCABULARY WORDS (BUT NOT TOO MANY!)

As you read through your chosen informational text, classify the words you think your students might struggle with into two categories: those which are "general academic words" and those which are more domain or discipline specific and used less frequently (Common Core 2010b, 33; Beck, McKeown, and Kucan 2013, 9).

Once you have made your lists, select the words that you think are most essential to your students' comprehension of the informational text and to supporting their ability to make meaningful connections with your core

33

content. However, be sure not to choose too many words; you're doing this to boost your students' engagement and confidence in reading the informational text, not to make it seem more onerous and formidable. Depending on the length and complexity of the text, between five and ten words is usually about right.

Most of the words you choose should be those academic words that your students will have the opportunity to use in their future academic work, which will reinforce their interest in and authentic learning of vocabulary.[1] We all hate having to learn a word we are never going to be able to use; in contrast, we love being able to show off a newly acquired and useful word!

However, especially if you are teaching this informational text in collaboration with a content-area teacher, be sure to take into account those domain- or discipline-specific terms that may be essential to his or her instructional goals, even if they are not used as widely. And, even if you are teaching this text on your own, you may still want to include a couple of the more specialized words if they are essential to understanding the meaning of the informational text.

For example, for the fruit flies article, we chose to focus on the following words: genetically modified, hypothesis, neurons, neuroscientist, suppresses, and tussles.

Hypothesis, suppresses, and tussles might be categorized as general academic words. Certainly, hypothesis is one of those words that we want to be using regularly in our literacy instruction in all the disciplines since it's the kind of academic language central to understanding and success across the content areas. In contrast, many students (and people) never encounter a neuroscientist or neuroscience, even if they benefit from the broader benefits in brain science. Still, they can't really make sense out of an article about fruit fly brains without understanding the key technical vocabulary here—neurons and genetically modified.

These six words are by no means the only ones that we thought might be unfamiliar to our students, but we determined that they were the words most essential to students being successful in comprehending the text and in articulating meaningful insights and connections related to our instructional goals.

CREATE PRE-READING ACTIVITIES THAT FRONT-LOAD BOTH KEY VOCABULARY AND CONCEPTS

For the sake of emphasis, we would like to first state what the next step is NOT: The next step is NOT to give the list of words to your students, have them look up and write down the definitions for them, and then have them use the words in sentences. None of that will help you build their confidence and interest in reading the informational text!

Your students will likely go through such an exercise, as they may unfortunately be accustomed to doing, dutifully and so disengaged intellectually that they may not even recognize having seen the words before when they encounter them in the informational text.

In contrast, we want to emphasize that your task in this step is twofold: to build your students' confidence and to establish or reinforce purpose.

The way to do this is to create pre-reading activities that front-load both key vocabulary and key concepts from the informational text. By doing so, you will efficiently scaffold your students' success with the informational text: they will not only know the definition of the words they studied when they come across them in the text, but they will be better able to access how the words are being used in the text and how they articulate the key ideas of the text.

In the rest of this section, we will demonstrate a variety of pre-reading vocabulary activities that will help you achieve this task. They are also designed to develop the overall language and vocabulary-acquisition skills that the Common Core language standard identifies as key to student success in college and careers (2010, 51).

However, we are by no means suggesting that you must do all of these activities every time you teach an informational text (nor are we suggesting that each individual student needs to complete each and every question on his or her own—more on this below). Choose those that best suit your instructional goals, available time, and students' literacy needs at that particular moment.

The following examples are those we developed to use with the fruit flies article.

Textbox 5.1

Anchor Standards 4–6 for Language-Vocabulary Acquisition and Use
4. Determine or clarify the meaning of unknown and multiple-meaning words and phrases by using context clues.
5. Demonstrate understanding of figurative language, word relationships, and nuances in word meanings.
6. Acquire and use accurately a range of general and domain-specific words and phrases sufficient for reading, writing, speaking, and listening at the college- and career-readiness level; demonstrate independence in gathering vocabulary knowledge when considering a word or phrase important to comprehension or expression.

USING CONTEXT CLUES

When we teach vocabulary, expanding our students' mental dictionary is not our only goal. As the CCSS indicate, we want them to become more confident in and capable of discerning word meanings from context. This, of course, is not just because they will be assessed on these skills on standardized tests but also because we want students to practice becoming successful, independent readers who can use a variety of strategies to discern meaning, even when they are not able or inclined to look up the definition of a word. Here, we offer two types of context-clue activities.

In the first example below, we use the word multiple times in both statements and questions to help students determine the meaning from context clues. At the same time, we are giving students the opportunity to start thinking about a concept that will be key to understanding the informational text.

> *Directions*: Read the following sentences and use context clues to determine the meaning of the italicized words.
>
> The research began with a *hypothesis* about what causes aggression. The scientists tested their theory with experiments. Based on the context, what is a scientific *hypothesis*? Why do scientists need to test a *hypothesis* with experiments?

In this example, the words "theory" and "test," and of course "scientist," offer students key context clues to help them close in on what a hypothesis might be. At the same time, the vocabulary question here is priming the students for the reading: introducing the idea that the article is about a scientific hypothesis tested by experimental research.

While we want students to articulate in their own words their understanding of the word's meaning based on their analysis of the context clues, we also want to give them practice using this skill in the ways they might be asked to on standardized tests. We think this is strategically important. Students get to practice the format of the test(s) they might face, which demystifies the test, reduces anxiety, and improves performance.

In addition, we integrate our test-prep work into our regular curriculum, so that preparation for THE TEST (whatever that might be) doesn't mean stepping away from our regular curriculum and real learning and moving to worksheets about which neither we nor the students care.

The following example follows the two-part, multiple-choice format that appears on the Partnership for Assessment of Readiness for College and Careers (PARCC) tests (2013). Context-clue questions are also featured on the Smarter Balanced assessments, but they generally include only questions like part A of the following exercise.

Directions: Here your task is to use context clues to understand the word's meaning.

Part A: The researchers tested *genetically modified* fruit flies that had been engineered so that their neurons would react to a certain temperature in the environment. *Genetically modified* here means

   a. aggressive
   b. reactive
   c. scientifically altered
   d. professionally trained

Part B: Which word from the sentence above best helps the reader understand the meaning of *genetically modified*?

   a. engineered
   b. react
   c. researchers
   d. environment

In Part A, the word "engineered" helps to suggest the correct answer as "C" or "scientifically altered."

It's important as you craft the wrong answer choices that you make sure that they are not too easy (i.e., obviously wrong) or not too hard (i.e., too close to the correct answer).

"Aggressive" and "reactive" are both words that could be used to describe fruit flies. Either could be substituted into the sentence without being obviously wrong.

Reactive also plays off the word "react," and students will often fall for a wrong answer simply because it looks like another word in the sentence.

And certainly scientists could genetically modify a fruit fly to make it more aggressive or reactive, but they could also genetically modify a fruit fly to make it gentle or passive.

Another way to think about the wrong answers here is to focus on the fact that the word "modified" is a past tense verb, which indicates that something has been done or has happened, which aligns with the context clue "engineered." If a student recognizes this context clue, then he or she would eliminate the first two answer choices because they don't contain anything that suggests any kind of action happening in the past.

That leaves choices "C" and "D," but "D" can be eliminated if the student thinks about what it means to "engineer" something, which is to alter the makeup or structure of something, not to train it. Though some answer choices can be eliminated quickly, students should have to think through each answer choice to come up with the right answer.

Part B, moreover, offers the student an additional clue to finding the right answer for the first, and this style of question demonstrates why preparation in the test format is so important for success on any test. Students need to understand that these paired questions need to be completed together: that Part B should be read before Part A is answered. Though the Smarter Balanced assessments (2013) do not feature two-part questions like these, they still ask students to demonstrate how they are using context clues to understand word meanings.

Theoretically, a student can rephrase the question as follows, what does it mean that these fruit flies were genetically modified? It means they were engineered to be different in some way. When they were engineered, the flies were scientifically altered.

We also really like this style of question because it requires the student to demonstrate her thinking by indicating the context clue used to answer the first question; in a sense this follow-up question requires the student to show her work, much like she might be asked to do in math or science class. The reasoning process becomes almost as important as the right answer.

These two types of context-clue questions, then, give students the opportunity to practice the skill of using context clues to determine word meanings, and, like all of the exercises in this section, can simultaneously be used to activate students' knowledge and get them thinking about key concepts they will encounter in the informational text.

USE THE DICTIONARY

So, most of us don't use the dictionary on a regular basis when we read. We use context clues, and that's why we ask our students to practice that skill above.

But sometimes we do turn to the dictionary. We know as teachers (and readers), and as indicated by the CCSS for literacy, that being able to use a dictionary as a tool in making meaning from a word or phrase in a text is an essential skill.

It seems like a simple task, right?

It isn't! It is a bewildering and frustrating task for students. Using the dictionary is harder than it seems.

Students need to have this skill, so having them look up definitions to unfamiliar words is an important first step, but what happens after that needs to be different from what has traditionally happened in both English and content-area classrooms. Simply having students copy down the definition and write a sentence using the word, and perhaps quizzing them on it later will not help them much toward owning the word. As mentioned above, this traditional process does nothing positive in terms of enhancing engagement, and also often does not produce terribly satisfying results even in terms of students' immediate ability to use the words.

Though less constrained by space considerations than in the pre-Internet age, dictionary definitions are often not terribly student-friendly (Beck, McKeown, and Kucan 2013, 43). They sometimes contain other words that students don't know, and therefore looking up the definition for one or more other words is often required to then come back and piece together the definition of the original word.

Even when this is not the case, using the dictionary usually requires significant language awareness and adeptness to take a terse definition and use it to make sense of a word in a particular context. As written, the dictionary definition likely will not fill in the blank easily or gracefully if students attempt simply to substitute it for the vocabulary word. Students need practice that helps them develop more nuanced skills in using dictionary definitions to make meaning.

Even the fact that electronic dictionaries contain multiple model sentences, a wonderful improvement over the basic and confusing definition-only dictionaries, makes our job harder. Our students rely too much on these model sentences. Either they copy them wholesale, which means they have not attempted to apply the word themselves; or they copy them in part, and then their sentences are awkward and/or often reveal misconceptions, ranging from slight to glaring.

For all of the above reasons discussed, when we push students immediately from looking up a definition to using the word in a sentence without further support, the outcome will likely be unsatisfying and not terribly useful for both teachers and students.

While we can blame the dictionary, we should reflect on our instructional techniques to address this common pedagogical challenge.

Take heart; there is another way.

In the example below, students are asked to look up the vocabulary words in the dictionary, but then to use the definitions they find to answer authentic, meaningful questions.

> *Directions*: Use the dictionary to look up the italicized words and answer the following questions based on their definitions.
> Some people argue that the *neurons* in teenagers' brains don't always work the way they should. Why would someone say that? Do you think your *neurons* work well? Why or why not?

This kind of prompt gives students "instructional contexts" (Beck 2013, 4) that use student-friendly language to support them in applying the definitions they have just accessed in ways that are both meaningful in terms of ideas and correct in terms of syntax. The potential result of a question like this is that students can engage in verbal tussles with each other about how their neurons work: "I think my neurons work just as well as my dad's, if not better. He can't even remember what he ate for breakfast!"

Furthermore, the context provided in these prompts also helps steer students toward the desired definition when a word has multiple definitions or connotations. Students are often thrown off course when reading a text that uses a common word in an uncommon way. Take, for instance, this question based on the Gorman article:

> *Directions*: Use the dictionary in order to understand the uncommon meaning of this common word.
>
> Gorman writes that, "When these neurons were *silenced*, the researchers were able to decrease aggression." These neurons weren't shushed or kept from making noise. What does *silenced* mean in this instance? How do you think neurons can be *silenced*?

We all know what silence means or even what it means to silence a noisy child, but this question asks the students to go to the dictionary in order to try to figure out how else the word silenced can be used. With our focus here on a relatively straightforward word used in an unusual way, we can focus on the students' dictionary skills *and* enhance their word knowledge.

Again, these types of questions help support success and engagement with the informational text because students have begun to really use the words and thus are primed both for confident understanding of how the word will be used specifically in the reading and, again, for purposeful thinking about the key concepts in the informational text.

PRACTICE USING THE WORD CORRECTLY

To truly own a new word, students need to know not just its definition but also how to apply the different forms in which it might appear. We can give students this kind of practice quickly and easily with questions like the following.

> *Directions*: Choose the correct form of the word that best fits in the blank within the following sentences.
>
> The principal has _____ that if students are well fed, they will do better on their schoolwork. He plans to test his _____ by offering good breakfasts to all students.

a. hypothesis . . . hypothesize
b. hypothesized . . . hypothesis
c. hypothesized . . . hypothesize
d. hypothesis . . . hypothesization

Questions like these—most likely used after an activity in which students determined the word's definition through use of context clues or the dictionary—help students quickly become more adept at using the vocabulary word and support their developing awareness of word forms and parts of speech (2010b, 51).

Textbox 5.2

CCSS.ELA-LITERACY.L.4b.9-12: Identify and correctly use patterns of word changes that indicate different meanings or parts of speech.

Note that this example does not explicitly address the use of fruit fly experiments and hypotheses, but it still reinforces the word's meaning by including ideas about testing hypotheses that relate to the informational text. It's important to use more familiar language and context in a question like this because this allows the students to focus specifically on using word forms correctly in a more normal conversational context in which they aren't, for example, discussing scientific experimentation.

VOCABULARY SKITS

We've saved the best for last. Vocabulary skits are a fun, quick, creative way for students "to get students actively involved in using and thinking about word meanings and creating lots of associations among words" (Beck, McKeown, and Kucan 2013, 83). And each step of the process is enormously valuable.

Getting students up on their feet and willing to risk being wrong in front of their peers is no small challenge, especially the first time. So, as with the word-form exercises above, we remove all of the other hurdles that might inhibit their confidence in creating and performing their vocabulary skit. We provide the definition of the word, multiple sample sentences using the word, and a scenario to serve as the basis for the skit. (As your students become more comfortable with creating the skits, you might allow them to come up with their own scenarios.)

Directions: Use the model sentences and definitions to understand the italicized word. Create a skit in which you address the given topic. Every member of the group must use the vocabulary word at least once during your performance of the skit.

Tussle—to have a fight; a fight, brawl, scuffle

- I think men are more likely to get into *tussles* than women.
- My father always wants to *tussle* with me about my chores, but I am doing the best I can.
- The endless *tussles* in Congress would be amusing if they didn't have such important implications for our future.

Scenario: Create a skit in which a group of scientists discuss the relationship between gender and aggression. Are men naturally more aggressive than women? Are women less likely to get into *tussles* than men? (Feel free to have the scientists get into a verbal [but not physical] *tussle* during their conversation.)

The students need to create the dialogue for the skit so that each member of the group uses the assigned vocabulary word at least once. The conversation they have in doing so gives them the opportunity to start using the word (ideally in multiple forms, if applicable) within their own group, before having to do so in front of the class.

Then, when each group gets up and performs its skit, the rest of the class gets to hear the word used over and over in a variety of ways, in a matter of minutes. Finally, listening to the discussions/rehearsal as well as the skits gives the teacher the chance to clarify any misconceptions in meaning or usage immediately. All of this leads to the kind of "massive practice" (Moffett and Wagner 1991, 10) that helps students create a cluster of associations that will help them own and use the word effectively.

PICK AND CHOOSE

We said we were going to show you how to make vocabulary a rewarding opportunity rather than a daunting challenge. After reading through all of these vocabulary activities, you may be feeling daunted again, but please take heed of this very important caveat: we are in no way, shape, or form suggesting that you have to or should do all of these activities all of the time.

Pick and choose those best suited for your instructional goals and your students' needs. If your students need practice with context clues, focus on those; if their context-clue skills are strong, focus on the dictionary or word form activities. But whenever possible, do the vocabulary skits!

TAKE TIME FOR VOCABULARY

Seriously, do not skip this step.

Keep in mind that using a range of rich and engaging vocabulary exercises does not need to take up a huge amount of class time. Each student does not need to tackle each vocabulary question independently in order for this to work!

Have groups of students work together to tackle different types of questions. Each group can share out their answers and their thinking with the whole class. And when you get to the text itself, each responsible group can be relied on to help with the different vocabulary words.

Or, for those vocabulary skills like dictionary work that the students find most tricky, use some teacher-led whole-class instruction where you model for your students, and then let them go off to practice in pairs or groups.

Eventually, yes, your students can do this work independently as homework, but don't shortchange the class review, which significantly contributes to the "massive practice" (Moffett and Wagner 1991, 10). And work toward an even more significant goal: have your students create their own vocabulary questions for their peers. This kind of exercise demonstrates real mastery, but it may take a long time to develop.

Remember, even if your students are strong, independent readers, they need practice developing these vocabulary skills. And even if you think the vocabulary in your chosen informational text isn't so challenging, there will likely be words and phrases that your students will struggle to make meaning from, based on the discipline-specific way they are used and/or the author's writing style. Without the right kind of preparation, that kind of stumbling block can dramatically and quickly undermine students' engagement and confidence.

NOTES

1. Appendix A of the Common Core literacy standards stresses the importance of offering instructional support for acquiring and using general academic, or "Tier Two," words, as well as the domain-specific, or "Tier Three," words: "Because Tier Three words are obviously unfamiliar to most students, contain the ideas necessary to a new topic, and are recognized as both important and specific to the subject area in which they are instructing students, teachers often define Tier Three words prior to

students encountering them in a text and then reinforce their acquisition throughout a lesson. Unfortunately, this is not typically the case with Tier Two words, which by definition are not unique to a particular discipline and as a result are not the clear responsibility of a particular content area teacher. What is more, many Tier Two words are far less well defined by contextual clues in the texts in which they appear and are far less likely to be defined explicitly within a text than are Tier Three words. Yet Tier Two words are frequently encountered in complex written texts and are particularly powerful because of their wide applicability to many sorts of reading. Teachers thus need to be alert to the presence of Tier-Two words and determine which ones need careful attention" (Common Core 2010b, 33).

REFERENCES

Beck, Isabel L., Margaret G. McKeown, and Linda Kucan. 2013. *Bringing Words to Life: Robust Vocabulary Instruction.* 2nd ed. New York: Guilford.

Common Core State Standards Initiative. 2010a. *Common Core State Standards for English Language Arts and Literacy in History/Social Studies, Science, and Technical Subjects.* Washington, DC: Common Core State Standards Initiative.

Common Core State Standards Initiative. 2010b. Appendix A to *Common Core State Standards for English Language Arts and Literacy in History/Social Studies, Science, and Technical Subjects.* Washington, DC: Common Core State Standards Initiative.

Fisher, Douglas, and Nancy Frey. 2015. "Meaningful Vocabulary Learning." *Culturally Diverse Classrooms* 72.6, 77–78. http://www.ascd.org/publications/educational-leadership/mar15/vol72/num06/Meaningful-Vocabulary-Learning.aspx.

Gorman, James. 2014. "To Study Aggression: A Fight Club for Flies." *The New York Times,* February 3. http://www.nytimes.com/2014/02/04/science/to-study-aggression-a-fight-club-for-flies.html.

Moffett, James, and Betty J. Wagner. 1991. *Student-Centered Language Arts, K-12.* New York: Heinemann.

Partnership for Assessment of Readiness for College and Careers. 2013. "PARCC Task Prototypes and New Sample Items for ELA/Literacy." http://www.parcconline.org/samples/ELA.

Smarter Balanced Assessment Consortium. 2013. "Sample Items and Performance Tasks." http://www.smarterbalanced.org/sample-items-and-performance-tasks/.

Chapter 6

Supporting Active Reading

Now that we have our students primed for success with our pre-reading vocabulary work, we must continue to support their active engagement as they read the informational text. Remember, one of the challenges in incorporating informational text into our instruction is that our students are not used to reading them. We can't assume that students will automatically know how they should interpret a news article as opposed to an editorial, let alone understand the various parts of a scientific study.

As reading specialist Cris Tovani (2000) notes, "Reading is thinking" (18). To be successful in reading an informational text, students need support that will help them notice and consider the details that will help them understand the text and how to place it within the context of their existing knowledge and other texts they have studied.

This kind of support is key for reluctant readers who may decode words fairly well, but struggle to comprehend what they read (Tovani 15), especially when we are challenging them with a complex informational text that may present a daunting range of unfamiliar vocabulary, syntax, and textual features in addition to the new concepts it contains.

CREATE GUIDED READING QUESTIONS

After you have cut your informational text, read through it carefully and create discussion questions that lead students to notice and articulate key concepts and textual features. Incorporate these into a sidebar alongside the text so that you can use them to guide your students' reading of the text (see

Table 6.1). These questions should require students to think and use evidence from the text in formulating their answers; the students shouldn't be able to just scan the text to find the answer.

Thanks to your pre-reading vocabulary activities, students will already have at least some sense of purpose when you present the informational text itself. But even then, students are sometimes inclined to speed through a reading as quickly and with as little thinking as possible.

So the purpose of your guided reading questions is to slow them down and make them consider what they are reading, so that they discover the key ideas that the informational text has to offer and make meaningful connections with their prior knowledge. We want students reading deeply, not just skimming the surface. By guiding the students and scaffolding the reading process for them with some focused reading prompts, you are strengthening the critical thinking skills that will help them become more confident and successful readers.

When you first start using informational texts like this in your class, be sure to model this kind of thoughtful reading yourself by voicing aloud your thinking process as you read, perhaps answering the first discussion question or two or the first guided reading question of a particular type (see the four types outlined in Table 6.1), and modeling how to annotate the text as well.

We like to make copies of our informational texts with big margins for the sidebars (see Table 6.1), so that students can jot down answers to the questions as well as annotate generally, noting interesting bits of information, additional questions, key pieces of evidence, etc.

Table 6.1 Using informational text template

SHORT INTRODUCTION TO THE TEXT (optional)	READING and DISCUSSION QUESTION TYPES
	Reflect on aspects of craft and structure (title, headers, captions, the type of informational text under consideration, the purpose, source, etc.).
	Vocabulary: Follow up your pre-reading vocabulary exercises with discussion of how key words are used in the informational text.
INFORMATIONAL TEXT GOES HERE (remember, feel free to cut any parts of the text that stray from your instructional goals)	**Key idea:** Draw attention to key ideas. Ask students to put these in their own words.
	Notice key details and ask students how they contribute to the text's overall meaning, purpose, or argument.

As your students become more accustomed to this kind of reading practice, you can differentiate instruction by assigning particular questions to particular students or groups of students. If it makes sense for the particular type of informational text you are using, you can also jigsaw the reading and assign each section and its guided reading questions to particular groups, who can then report back their findings to the whole class. Again, having all students take notes in the sidebar gives them a purpose as they listen to their peers' contributions.

Finally, as your students develop an overall comfort level with this type of exercise, have them develop the sidebar prompts. Again, this can be done in groups for particular sections, and then groups or the class as a whole can tackle these student-generated questions. As with student-generated multiple-choice or vocabulary questions, this level of engagement with the material and the reading strategy is the ultimate demonstration of mastery. And if the work is done in groups, all your students don't have to have reached full competence at this level in order for the exercise to be successful.

TYPES OF GUIDED READING QUESTIONS

Your guided reading questions should serve at least these four key purposes:

1. *Reflect* on aspects of craft and structure (title, headers, captions, the type of informational text under consideration, the purpose, source, etc.). Students need guidance in making sense of the textual features, some of which may be very specific to the particular discipline in question, especially when they first encounter a particular type of informational text. Knowing how to interpret these features is key to their successful comprehension.

To Study Aggression, a Fight Club for Flies
By JAMES GORMAN
The New York Times
FEB. 3, 2014

Males' aggression toward each other is an old story throughout the animal kingdom. It's not that females aren't aggressive, but in many species, male-on-male battles are more common.

Reflect on the title. What do you think the article will be about? Have you ever heard of a fight club? Would you expect flies to have a fight club?

Reflect on the kind of informational text. Where and when was this article published? What does that tell you? What do you think the purpose of the article is? How reliable do you think the information is?

Figure 6.1 Reflect on Craft and Structure.

In the example above, the prompts for active reading and thinking begin with the title of the article. The first set of questions activates students' existing knowledge to predict what the reading will be about and to reinforce purpose. The second set of questions asks students to think about the type of text they are reading and what they can determine about its reliability based on where and when it was published.

2. *Vocabulary*: Follow up your pre-reading vocabulary exercises with discussion of how the words are used in the informational text (Figure 6.2).

Take fruit flies. "The males are more aggressive than females," said David J. Anderson, a California Institute of Technology *neuroscientist* who knows their *tussles* well. Dr. Anderson runs a kind of fight club for fruit flies in his lab at Caltech, with the goal of understanding the deep evolutionary roots of very fundamental behaviors.

Dr. Anderson, Kenta Asahina and a group of their colleagues recently identified one gene and a tiny group of *neurons,* sometimes as few as three, present only in the brains of male fruit flies, that can control aggression.

Vocabulary: If David Anderson is a neuroscientist, what does he study? Given the fact that the paragraph discusses fruit flies, what else can you tell about Dr. Anderson's research?

Vocabulary: The article suggests that Anderson "knows their tussles well." Put this into your own words. Who is tussling here? What does it mean for Anderson to "know their tussles"?

Figure 6.2   How are Key Vocabulary Words Used?

It's important to follow up with questions like these to give students the opportunity to apply their new vocabulary knowledge in an authentic context and to be sure they can use their vocabulary knowledge to support their understanding of key ideas in the text.

3. *Key idea*: One of the most difficult aspects of reading complex text is identifying the main ideas (and distinguishing between main ideas and supporting details). Help your students with this skill by drawing their attention to the key ideas that you identify for them. Ask students to put these into their own words (Figure 6.3).

Key Idea: The research began with "the hypothesis that neuropeptides, which are a kind of hormone in the brain, had a role in controlling aggression. Put this into your own words. What was the hypothesis for the research?

Key idea: How did the scientists use genetic modifications in their experiments? What did they discover? What is tachykinin and why is it important?

The research began, Dr. Anderson said, with the *hypothesis* that neuropeptides, which are a kind of hormone in the brain, had a role in controlling aggression.

To find out which neuropeptides were important, the team tested different lines, of *genetically modified* fruit flies. All lines had been engineered so that at a certain temperature, around 80 degrees, a chemical change would make specific neurons fire. In each line the neurons were different. They tested about 40 lines of flies, raising the temperature to increase the firing of neurons and determine which flies showed increased aggressive behavior. They used another technique to make neurons they were studying become fluorescent green so they could see their anatomy and location.

Figure 6.3   Identifying Key Ideas.

Notice that the questions here ask students to build upon their new vocabulary knowledge in order to put the key ideas in the text into their own words. Again, these types of questions are making the students really think about what they are reading. When we ask in the second set of questions why tachykinin is important, we are basically asking the students to articulate why this is a key idea in the text. Answering these questions helps students understand the text while simultaneously building their language and comprehension skills generally.

4. *Notice*: Ask students to notice key details and ask students how they contribute to the text's overall meaning, purpose, or argument.

| In the end, they clearly established that a significant behavioral difference in male and female flies was based in the brain. What this might mean for humans is unclear. A drug that *suppresses* the activity of substance P in humans had, at one time, seemed very promising as an antidepressant. It failed in clinical trials, but Dr. Anderson and his co-authors suggested in the Cell paper that it might be tested for symptoms like uncontrollable anger that can affect people with illnesses like post-traumatic stress syndrome. | **Notice** that the article suggests that "What this might mean for humans is unclear." What does that mean? What claims are the scientists making about aggression in fruit flies? Can they make any claims, based on the research, about aggression in humans? What are the implications of the research for the study of substance P? |

Figure 6.4   Ideas or Sentences that Merit Extended Discussion.

Sometimes a relatively simple sentence, buried within the details of a complex paragraph, offers a bombshell of an idea that requires serious consideration. In the example above, "What this might mean for humans is unclear" is just such a bombshell. There's nothing tricky about the sentence itself, but the ideas within the sentence require discussion. This question ensures that students don't gloss over a relatively simple but key sentence and gives them the opportunity to extend their thinking, in this instance to put the conclusions of the article into context and evaluate their significance.

OPTIONAL LAST STEP: WRITE A SHORT INTRODUCTION TO THE TEXT

After you have created your sidebar questions, you may want to write a short introduction to the text, especially if the text itself or its subject matter is particularly complex. The introduction might include information about the author and/or the occasion or historical context for when the text was written. It can also provide some guidance to students in thinking about the particular type of text and how they should interpret it.

For example, if the text is a scientific study, you might want to explain who the researchers are and give a little information about their prominence in their field. In the case of a Supreme Court decision, you may want to provide some of the historical context surrounding the decision. If you are collaborating with a colleague from another discipline, you should do this step together to make sure that the introduction frames the informational text in terms of each of your respective instructional goals and disciplinary concerns.

Writing up this sort of introduction and including it for our students allows their reading to be the central element of discovery about the text/topic. Instead of beginning with a lecture, which foregrounds your expertise and their ignorance, the introduction gives them the tools to do the reading and thinking on their own (but of course under your guidance).

NOW WHAT?

You have found and prepared your informational text. You have prepared your students and have guided them through a successful reading. In the next chapters, we will talk about what kinds of activities to engage in to capitalize on all of the rich reading and thinking your students have done.

REFERENCES

Gorman, James. 2014. "To Study Aggression: A Fight Club for Flies." *The New York Times*, February 3. http://www.nytimes.com/2014/02/04/science/to-study-aggression-a-fight-club-for-flies.html.

Tovani, Cris. 2000. *I Read It, But I Don't Get It: Comprehension Strategies for Adolescent Readers*. Portland, ME: Stenhouse.

Chapter 7

Checking for Understanding

THE REALITY OF STANDARDIZED ASSESSMENTS

If you live in a universe free from the realities of standardized assessments, then you can skip over this chapter. But we doubt that universe is densely populated (or populated at all). Even if you teach at a private school exempt from the mandate of standardized assessments, your students still face myriad multiple-choice exams throughout their educational lifetime and beyond. There are the SATs, the ACTs, the GREs, the driving test, licensing exams in numerous professions, etc.

We all live in this world.

And there are two elements to that world that we think are particularly important to the project of using informational text across the disciplines.

First, test preparation, gaining familiarity with the format of a test and also with some of the basics of general test-taking, works. That's why test preparation is an enormous, highly profitable industry.

We don't want our classrooms to turn into test-prep factories, but we also want to prepare our students, especially those who don't have the resources for fancy test preparation classes, for the realities of standardized assessments. After all, we want our students to succeed.

Second, many of those assessments are coming into alignment with the Common Core, particularly in terms of using informational text readings from across the disciplines as their base.

We can incorporate a little standardized test preparation into our teaching of these informational texts while also pursuing our content area and curriculum goals. That way, hopefully, our students will be a little more prepared for the standardized test universe they face, and we won't have to spend days or weeks away from our curriculum in the mind-numbing world of test preparation.

HOW TO DO THIS WORK?

We think your use of multiple-choice questions to check for understanding in relation to your informational text should be as short and painless as possible. Our template below, based on the general organization of the Common Core and of the current PARCC and Smarter Balanced assessments, addresses vocabulary in context, key ideas and details, integration of knowledge and ideas, and craft and structure.

Remember that mastering this genre of multiple-choice questions requires literacy skills and test-taking skills, so your work in this area should combine both elements. In addition, remember that students who do poorly on these types of assessments may have the underlying content knowledge and understanding of the text, but the multiple-choice assessment may limit their ability to demonstrate that knowledge.

This is, of course, why we use multiple measures of assessment, but it's also why this exercise is important. We don't want these students to be discouraged by multiple-choice assessments; at the same time, we do want to build their test-taking skills.

Susan's students, for example, struggle with these sorts of tests and questions, so Audrey did some whole-class instruction in which she modeled the thought process behind attacking multiple-choice questions. She talked about reading all of the answers, eliminating wrong answers, reading both parts of paired questions before attempting to answer, etc.

It's worth noting that Susan's students also struggled with the questions that require test takers to select more than one correct answer. This is a relatively new type of standardized test question, and it's cropping up on all sorts of tests. It's very different from the kind where you pick the one best answer because you cannot employ the elimination of wrong answers technique, so explicit practice on how to tackle this type of question is very valuable.

Move from this kind of whole-class, guided work to small-group work, where the students join together to tackle the questions. Again, if you remember that your goal is both assessment of their understanding of the text and improvement of their test-taking skills, the time taken to do group work on these kinds of questions makes sense.

When ready, of course, it's reasonable to use multiple-choice questions as quizzes or homework to check for understanding.

Think also, however, about building toward real mastery by having your students practice making up answers to your or their own questions, complete with right and wrong answers. This kind of exercise, completed individually or in teams, will move your students even further toward both demonstrating their understanding of the informational text and building their confidence with standardized assessments.

TYPES OF MULTIPLE-CHOICE QUESTIONS

Vocabulary in Context

Remember that these questions can focus on familiar or unfamiliar words or phrases, and they should always focus on the student's ability to determine the word's or phrase's meaning from context. This type of question should never depend on general vocabulary knowledge.

A. In "To Study Aggression," James Gorman explains that "all lines had been engineered so that at a certain temperature, around 80 degrees, a chemical change would make specific neurons fire . . . they narrowed the search to neurons that were producing the neuropeptide tachykinin." By "fire," Gorman here means

   a. explode
   b. combust
   c. produce tachykinin
   d. become very hot

B. Which word(s) from the sentence above best help(s) the reader understand the meaning of "fire" in this context?

   a. 80 degrees
   b. certain temperature
   c. producing the neuropeptide
   d. engineered

In this example, a broader reading of the section in question, beyond what is reprinted in question A, will help students understand the answers to both A and B. Outside knowledge of what the word "fire" means here is minimally important; instead, the questions ask students to think about how "fire" is being used in this context. Notice that the incorrect answers (a) and (b) to question B both link back to the general but incorrect use of the word "fire."

You may or may not want to construct this sort of question using the paired format, but if you do, remind students that they should use the question and answers in the second question to help them answer the first.

Key Ideas and Details

These two-part questions, to us, represent one of the signal emphases of the Common Core: the use of evidence. The question in part A is familiar and unsurprising—the sort of question we've seen on standardized assessments for years. It's the second question that's innovative. It asks students to back up their thinking (Textbox 7.1).

Textbox 7.1

> **According to the Common Core State Standards, "Students Who Are College and Career Ready in Reading, Writing, Speaking, Listening, and Language ... value evidence":** "Students cite specific evidence when offering an oral or written interpretation of a text. They use relevant evidence when supporting their own points in writing and speaking, making their reasoning clear to the reader or listener, and they constructively evaluate others' use of evidence" (2010, 7).

The nice thing about this set of questions is that it minimizes the guessing. Instead, it asks students to justify their response in A through specific details from the text. In our example below, the details are direct quotations from the text. Again, reading through the answers in Part B sends students back into the text itself and helps them answer Part A. And if the student can't find THREE pieces of evidence in Part B to support his/her answer in Part A, that's the tip-off that the answer for Part A is probably incorrect.

A. Which of the following sentences best state the main idea of "To Study Aggression"?

  a. Men are more aggressive than women.
  b. The brains of fruit flies are like the brains of mammals.
  c. Studying aggression in male fruit flies may help us understand aggression in humans.
  d. Substance P seems to be the key to understanding aggression.

B. Select the THREE pieces of evidence from the article that BEST support your answer to question 3.

  a. They could even make small flies attack bigger flies.
  b. A drug that suppresses the activity of substance P in humans had, at one time, seemed very promising as an antidepressant.

c. Studying aggression in fruit flies can actually teach us something about some of the molecules that control aggression.
d. It is clear that humans and flies have more in common than it might appear.
e. The research began, Dr. Anderson said, with the hypothesis that neuropeptides, which are a kind of hormone in the brain, had a role in controlling aggression.
f. When they compared the brains of male and female flies, they found a few neurons, present only in the male, that produced tachykinin.
g. But it is a striking indication of how brain structure and chemistry work together, as well as a reminder that as different as humans and flies are, they are not always very far apart.
h. Males' aggression toward each other is an old story.

Integration of Knowledge and Ideas

This type of question asks students to think critically about the reading and make inferences beyond what's right there in the text.

Which question is unanswered by the reading?

a. Why are men more aggressive than women?
b. What role do neuropeptides have in relationship to aggression?
c. What makes male fruit flies more aggressive than female fruit flies?
d. What kind of behavior is linked with substance P?

The question here requires students to distinguish between the sorts of questions that are directly and explicitly answered by the text and those that are not. In this case, the scientists are clearly interested in the issue of male versus female aggression, but the experiments under discussion here focus on fruit flies and extrapolation about human behavior is not justified by the experiments or suggested by the article.

Craft and Structure

These questions are particularly interesting for cross-disciplinary readings in which students need to think about text types and text structure. How, for example, does an illustration, a chart, or a caption contribute to the overall argument of the text? What is the function of one particular section—the opening or the closing, for example—in relation to the overall text?

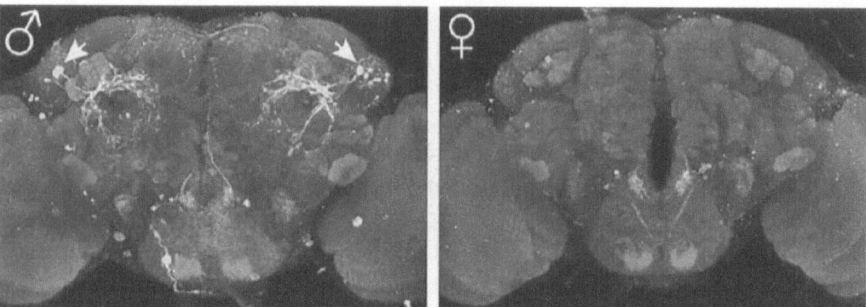

Figure 7.1 At Caltech, researchers identified a gene and a tiny group of neurons in male flies that control aggression. Left, a male fruit fly's brain. The arrows point to the neurons that the female brain lacks. Photo: Kenta Asahina

What is the function of the illustration in the article?

a. to make the article easier to read
b. to offer a visual illustration of the difference between male and female fruit fly brains
c. to explain male aggression
d. to show how similar male and female fruit fly brains are

Getting students to think about how different types of text employ different textual features is one of the opportunities and challenges of this cross-disciplinary enterprise. We know that students often don't know how to read these different text features (sometimes they skip right over them). These sorts of questions ask them to think critically not just about the argument in a text but also about how that argument is constructed, put together, and presented.

PARCC/SMARTER BALANCED QUESTION TYPES REFERENCE SHEET

Use this sheet as a quick reference when writing PARCC/SB-style or other standardized-test questions. Note that most multiple-choice questions on the PARCC assessments consist of two parts.

VOCABULARY IN CONTEXT

PART A OPTIONS

- What is the meaning of X as used in this sentence/paragraph?
- Which word is a synonym for X as it is used in the text?

PART B OPTIONS

- Which phrase from the sentence/paragraph best helps the reader understand the meaning of X?
- Which idea provides the best context for determining the meaning of X?
- Besides the sentence that contains the word/phrase mentioned in Part A, select the other sentence in paragraph X that helps the reader understand the meaning of X.
- Which phrase helps the reader understand the meaning of X?
- Which quotation helps clarify the meaning of X?
- Which language feature provides context for determining the meaning of X? (e.g., rather signals contrast, finally emphasizes importance, etc.)

KEY IDEAS AND DETAILS

PART A OPTIONS

- What is the central idea(s) of the reading?
- Which two statements best summarize the theme/main idea of the text?
- What claim/argument does the author/text make?
- Which sentence provides an accurate summary of X (not the whole piece)?
- Which statement describes a similarity/difference between the two texts under discussion?

PART B OPTIONS

- Which sentence(s)/piece(s) of evidence from the text best support the answer to the question above?
- Choose two quotations/examples/pieces of evidence that support the answer to the question above.
- Which piece of evidence below does NOT support the answer to the question above?
- Which paragraph best supports the answer to Part A?

INTEGRATION OF KNOWLEDGE AND IDEAS

PART A OPTIONS

- Which question is unanswered by the reading?
- What is one question the article answers?

PART B OPTIONS

- Which statement is true and/or is answered by the reading related to the question above?
- Which quotation from the article best reflects an inference that supports the answer to Part A?

CRAFT AND STRUCTURE

PART A OPTIONS

- What is the function of sentence A/paragraph A?
- How does sentence A/paragraph A contribute to the theme/argument of the text?
- In this sentence/phrase/paragraph, the author writes X. Which paraphrase best explains the author's ideas/thinking here?
- How does the author structure the opening/closing, etc. to advance his/her argument?
- How does the author develop his claim that X?
- How does the reference to X help advance the argument as a whole?
- What is the main purpose of the text?
- How does the author use paragraph X to advance his overall argument? (criticizes opponents, produces a list of authorities, offers historical support, summarizes general argument)

PART B OPTIONS

- In what other section of the text is the idea of sentence A/paragraph A discussed?
- Where in the text are the ideas introduced in sentence A/paragraph A further developed?
- Which words/phrases/sentence in the text best help you understand the meaning of the phrase under consideration in the question above?
- Which example from the text illustrates the idea/meaning of the idea/thinking in the question above?
- Which statement from the opening/closing/etc. emphasizes the answer to Part A?
- Which quotation provides the best evidence for the answer to Part A?
- Which details (paired, one from each text) support the answer to Part A?
- In which sentence of paired text does the author use a similar technique?
- Which paragraph from the paired text makes a point similar to the answer in Part A?

REFERENCES

Common Core State Standards Initiative. 2010. *Common Core State Standards for English Language Arts and Literacy in History/Social Studies, Science, and Technical Subjects.* Washington, DC: Common Core State Standards Initiative.

Gorman, James. 2014. "To Study Aggression: A Fight Club for Flies." *The New York Times*, February 3. http://www.nytimes.com/2014/02/04/science/to-study-aggression-a-fight-club-for-flies.html.

Partnership for Assessment of Readiness for College and Careers. 2013. "PARCC Task Prototypes and New Sample Items for ELA/Literacy." http://www.parcconline.org/samples/ELA.

Smarter Balanced Assessment Consortium. 2013. "Sample Items and Performance Tasks." http://www.smarterbalanced.org/sample-items-and-performance-tasks/.

Chapter 8

Extending Learning
Writing and Discussion Activities

THE BIG PAYOFF

Having read and worked with the informational text, students are now ready for the big payoff: writing and discussion assignments that drive home the content-area connection.

Depending on the level of collaboration involved in your teaching of the informational text (whether or not you are co-teaching this article with another content-area teacher), you may want to think about two different kinds of discussion/writing tasks: one which focuses solely on the informational text and the second which puts the informational text in conversation with material from one of the content areas. One of you might choose to assign the former assignment; the other might use the latter.

For example, either a language arts teacher or a science teacher might ask students to consider the following question:

A. James Gorman discusses research on aggression in fruit flies by a group of scientists.

- Why, according to Gorman, are the scientists interested in aggression in fruit flies?
- What have these scientists discovered about aggression in fruit flies? What are the implications of their discoveries for humans? What questions remain unanswered by the research?

Use information *and textual evidence from the article* to support your response. Be sure to follow the conventions of standard English.

The question above is fairly generic. Of course a science teacher could modify it to focus on any particular area of interest:

- the process of scientific experimentation discussed in the article;
- the implications of the article for the connection between biology/neurology and social behavior;
- the issue of the relationship between scientific experimentation on animals and our understanding of humans.

All of these questions could allow students to demonstrate their specific understanding of the Gorman article together with some broader understanding of big scientific ideas/questions.

For the language arts teacher, however, question A above could easily be handled without substantial collaboration with a science teacher, even while allowing students to make cross-disciplinary connections and display knowledge across the disciplines that can make them feel smart. The more science-oriented questions above are probably too much for the language arts teacher to tackle on his/her own.

But, as we suggested at the outset, the Gorman fruit fly article has the potential to enliven discussion of *Lord of the Flies* for the language arts teacher.

> B. Use what you've learned about male fruit fly aggression in James Gorman's article in relation to the excerpt (the scene in which the boys attack and kill the sow) from William Golding's *Lord of the Flies*.
>
> - How might the scene from *Lord of the Flies* reflect the concerns about aggression in Gorman's article?
> - How might the scientists Gorman discusses analyze the behavior of the boys in the scene? If they could study the boys, what might they be interested in learning more about?
> - How does Gorman's discussion of male fruit fly aggression change the way you read this scene in *Lord of the Flies*? Do you find this a compelling way to think about this scene and/or the novel generally? Why or why not?
>
> Develop your essay *by providing textual evidence from both texts*. Be sure to follow the conventions of standard English.

Notice how this set of questions asks the students to make some really substantial intellectual moves, using their understanding of scientific experimentation and of the particulars of the research on male fruit flies and applying that understanding to the literary text. The exercise has the potential to draw the scientifically-inclined students more deeply into the literary text, and, vice versa, to draw the literature students into broader scientific questions.

At the very least, students who study this text in some way in both classes will be putting their content knowledge in each discipline into dialogue, even if the teachers aren't themselves able to participate in a co-teaching, simultaneous discussion. These students will be using this complex informational text, together with their content-area knowledge, to make sense out of their world—in this case, a small piece of the issue of male aggression.

However, be sure to explicitly state your intent to put the informational text into dialogue with the literary text or other content-area material, especially if it's from a different discipline. Though many students will automatically start making connections whether you ask them to or not, not all students will naturally do this. We have, unfortunately, so thoroughly indoctrinated students into the idea of separate disciplines through the traditional structure of our educational system that, as reading specialist Cris Tovani (2000) writes of her own daughter, "It never crossed her mind to use information in one class to help her in another" (65).

We know that the world isn't divided into discrete disciplines, so we need to help our students discover that. The Common Core asks students to put texts into dialogue, to draw evidence to support analysis and reflection, and to synthesize ideas and information. Students who use informational text across the disciplines more than meet these goals, and they do so while breaking down the artificial boundaries of our disciplines and classrooms.

REFERENCES

Gorman, James. 2014. "To Study Aggression: A Fight Club for Flies." *The New York Times*, February 3. http://www.nytimes.com/2014/02/04/science/to-study-aggression-a-fight-club-for-flies.html.

Tovani, Cris. 2000. *I Read It, But I Don't Get It: Comprehension Strategies for Adolescent Readers*. Portland, ME: Stenhouse.

Chapter 9

Thinking Big

Class Activities and Projects

We've reassured you throughout this book that you can start small while collaborating and incorporating informational text into your curriculum. And that's absolutely true. But, perhaps you and your collaborator are so excited by the informational text you've found and the connections you're making with your core content that you want to go BIG.

Sometimes your informational text lesson will just be a new stepping stone along the path of your existing unit, but sometimes the connections and concepts that the informational text evokes will lead your unit in a whole new direction and might inspire you to rethink whatever culminating activity or assessment you've used in the past.

If that's the case, we have some suggestions for how to craft a successful capstone project that will showcase—and even extend—the deep thinking and learning your students have been doing.

DYNAMIC, PURPOSEFUL REPRESENTATIONS OF LEARNING

In order to prepare our students for college and careers, we want to give them authentic opportunities to work collaboratively and to present their knowledge and ideas in writing as well as in non-written or non-narrative formats, using available technology as much as possible. But we hope it is clear that this cannot simply mean that students do a little independent research and then deliver a PowerPoint presentation.

Think about the real ways that the concepts and essential questions involved in your unit enter and influence local and/or national public conversations and how your students might create an authentic product that could

Textbox 9.1

> **CCSS.ELA-LITERACY.W.6:** Use technology, including the Internet, to produce and publish writing and to interact and collaborate with others.
>
> **CCSS.ELA-LITERACY.SL.1:** Prepare for and participate effectively in a range of conversations and collaborations with diverse partners, building on others' ideas and expressing their own clearly and persuasively.
>
> **CCSS.ELA-LITERACY.SL.2:** Integrate and evaluate information presented in diverse media and formats, including visually, quantitatively, and orally.
>
> **CCSS.ELA-LITERACY.SL.3:** Evaluate a speaker's point of view, reasoning, and use of evidence and rhetoric.
>
> **CCSS.ELA-LITERACY.SL.4:** Present information, findings, and supporting evidence such that listeners can follow the line of reasoning and the organization, development, and style are appropriate to task, purpose, and audience.
>
> **CCSS.ELA-LITERACY.SL.5:** Make strategic use of digital media and visual displays of data to express information and enhance understanding of presentations.
>
> **CCSS.ELA-LITERACY.SL.6:** Adapt speech to a variety of contexts and communicative tasks, demonstrating command of formal English when indicated or appropriate.

actually do so as well, both within your school and possibly beyond. Here are some ideas:

- Host and participate in a talk show/debate/panel discussion
- Prepare and deliver testimony for a mock (or real) school board meeting
- Create and publish a video news report or podcast
- Create an audio or video public service announcement
- Conduct a mock trial
- Conduct a survey and publicize the results as an infographic
- Create a website or social media campaign to raise awareness
- Design and conduct a workshop/training for peers and/or community members

This is where you can let the visual/spatial, auditory, kinesthetic, interpersonal, and logical learners you engaged at the beginning of your informational text unit/lesson shine. The goal is to give all of your students the opportunity to create meaningful representations of what they have learned during your unit—both in the discipline in which they may have previously excelled as well as the one in which they hopefully have developed newfound confidence and interest.

Their efforts will give you a product by which to assess their learning, and the process of creating the product will enhance both their disciplinary content knowledge and literacy skills. Taking the concepts they've learned and deciding how to represent them most effectively, according to the purposes and parameters of the project, is the real display of mastery in the disciplines for which we're always striving (Wilson and Chavez 2014).

CLASS ACTIVITY: TALK SHOW ON AGGRESSION IN FRUIT FLIES AND HUMANS

Here is a model class activity based on our fruit fly science-language arts collaboration. See Appendix A for a model rubric for this project.

Task: Your goal is to conduct a TV talk show debate around the question, "Is aggression genetic?" The discussion will incorporate the viewpoints of multiple guests, including scientists, experts on aggression, and one or more characters from *Lord of the Flies*. Each student will be required to determine (based on research and/or understanding of the texts read in class) how his/her character would act and speak during the debate.

Talk show host or cohosts: Prepares questions for both panelists and audience members. Acts as moderator for the debate, asking questions of the panelists and audience members and promoting balanced and civil discussion among all parties.

Panelists:

- James Gorman
- David J. Anderson, neuroscientist
- Piggy
- Jack
- William Golding
- Other characters from *Lord of the Flies*, as desired

Outside experts (these experts will be expected to offer evidence to back up their assertions about the origins of aggression):

- Outside experts on aggression in athletes
- Outside experts on aggression among girls
- Outside experts on cyberbullying

In addition, each student must produce the following:

1. *Explanation of character:* Write a reflective narrative in which you explain how you went about determining how your character would act, what he or she would say during the debate in response to particular questions, and how he or she would perceive and react to the other characters. Justify (with textual evidence) how your character's words and actions make sense based on your research and/or your understanding of *Lord of the Flies* and the fruit fly informational text and any additional research you might have consulted.
2. *Postdebate evaluation:* (1) Write a reflection in which you evaluate how the talk show debate was conducted. Discuss how well your classmates represented their characters: did their words and actions make sense for their roles? (2) Reflecting on the informational text readings, *Lord of the Flies*, yours and your peers' research, as well as the exchange of ideas during the debate, discuss the essential question: "Is aggression genetic?" How has your understanding of this question changed?

In this model project, students who take on the role of outside experts will seek out additional informational texts as research for their roles. This option offers substantial opportunity for differentiation. First of all, students have the opportunity to exert some preference in choosing their role. Second, since some roles require additional research, you can offer or assign these to students with particular reading strengths, to carefully selected pairs of students who can work together to unpack the new informational texts, or to individual students with whom you plan to work individually to offer additional support.

Regardless, you may want students to conduct their research completely independently, or you may want to provide suggested informational texts or resources for others.

For this particular project, some excellent outside sources from the *New York Times* include "The Playground Gets Even Tougher," a discussion of aggression among young girls; "Measuring Athletes' Level of Aggression" and "Athletes Struggle to Channel Aggressive Nature," two articles summarizing psychological assessments of aggression and impulse control in professional athletes; and "Mobs Are Born as Word Grows by Text Message," a report on social media being used to inspire increasingly aggressive and sometimes violent flash mobs in various cities. Students might also look at articles and videos about the Stanford Prison Experiment.

TAKE TIME TO REFLECT

After you've all basked in the glow of your students' inspiring and insightful projects, there is one last, critical step. Have each student write a reflective narrative discussing the work.

This reflective narrative can serve two different functions:

First, each student has an opportunity to explain the thinking behind the project, explaining his or her choices and/or those of his or her group/class in conducting the project, explaining how the decisions reflect the students' understanding of the issues and evaluating the final outcomes of the project, especially in terms of how they drew upon and represented their literacy skills and content-area knowledge from both of the disciplines involved.

This reflection supports your students' metacognitive development, provides a way to assess your students' individually, and gives your students the chance to spell out their thinking to you. There is nothing worse than a project that makes perfect sense to the students but that we find baffling in terms of how it addresses the tasks. Give your students the responsibility of making that connection clear to you.

Second, though this function may not be relevant to all types of projects (including the model above), the reflection can ask students to discuss the collaborative nature of the project. Here, each student can discuss not only which task(s) he/she took responsibility for but also how the collaborative process worked.

This is a moment for the student to go beyond identifying who did what (which is helpful so that you know every student was pulling his or her weight) to reflect broadly about their strengths and weaknesses as collaborative partners. These collaborative skills, after all, are central to success in college and career and need to be nurtured alongside literacy and content-area proficiency.

Finally, a narrative reflection is one more opportunity for your students to practice and enhance their literacy skills—a writing assignment disguised as a reflection. Be sure to work with your collaborative partner in establishing the requirements of the reflection narrative so that your respective disciplinary concerns are included.

LOGISTICS

Ideally, the capstone project will be a collaborative effort conducted across both classes involved, perhaps with a showcase of the students' projects after school. However, if one of the collaborating teachers cannot devote the time to such an undertaking, it can be conducted solely within the other teacher's class. The project will then likely focus on the content connections more specifically relevant to that discipline.

The project can be undertaken as a class or in smaller groups; either way, each student should have a clearly defined role.

Use a balanced approach to technology: Don't let your own technological skills (or lack thereof) unnecessarily limit your project ideas; on the other hand, don't assume that all of your students will naturally know how to use the technology. Be ready to provide or help them find resources that will enable them to acquire any necessary skills quickly and easily.

REFERENCES

Chenelle, Susan, and Audrey Fisch. 2015. "Text to Text: 'Lord of the Flies' and 'A Fight Club for Fruit Flies." *The New York Times Learning Network*, January 22. http://learning.blogs.nytimes.com/2015/01/22/text-to-text-lord-of-the-flies-and-a-fight-club-for-flies/comment-page-1/?_r=0.

Common Core State Standards Initiative. 2010. *Common Core State Standards for English Language Arts and Literacy in History/Social Studies, Science, and Technical Subjects.* Washington, DC: Common Core State Standards Initiative.

Dietz, Jeff. 2009. "Athletes Struggle to Channel Aggressive Nature." *The New York Times,* November 21. http://www.nytimes.com/2009/11/22/sports/22brain.html.

Dreifus, Claudia. 2007. "Finding Hope in Knowing the Universal Capacity for Evil." *The New York Times.* April 3. http://www.nytimes.com/2007/04/03/science/03conv.html.

Gorman, James. 2014. "To Study Aggression: A Fight Club for Flies." *The New York Times,* February 3. http://www.nytimes.com/2014/02/04/science/to-study-aggression-a-fight-club-for-flies.html.

Markowitz, Dan. 1996. "Measuring Athletes' Level of Aggression." *The New York Times,* September 22. http://www.nytimes.com/1996/09/22/nyregion/measuring-athletes-level-of-aggression.html.

Paul, Pamela. 2010. "The Playground Gets Even Tougher." *The New York Times,* October 8. http://www.nytimes.com/2010/10/10/fashion/10Cultural.html.

Urbina, Ian. 2010. "Mobs Are Born as Word Grows by Text Message." *The New York Times,* March 24. http://www.nytimes.com/2010/03/25/us/25mobs.html.

Wilson, Amy Alexandra, and Kathryn J. Chavez. 2014. *Reading and Representing Across the Content Areas: A Classroom Guide.* New York: Teachers College Press.

Zimbardo, Philip. G. 2015. *The Stanford Prison Experiment,* July 20. http://www.prisonexp.org/.

Chapter 10

Using Hooks
Multimedia

You have your informational text prepped. You've created engaging pre-reading vocabulary activities to prime your students for a successful reading experience. You've prepared check-for-understanding questions and writing and discussion prompts that will draw your students into making deep, meaningful observations about the informational text itself and connections with your core disciplinary content.

There's just one more thing left to do. But it will be fun; we promise.

You've done everything right in terms of setting your students up for success with your informational text, but we can't escape the fact that our students live in an audiovisual world. They are more comfortable in this environment, but it's an environment in which they also need to develop and hone their literacy and critical thinking skills. In addition, we also want to take into account the fact that many of our students are more naturally visual/spatial or auditory rather than linguistic learners and to be sure to support their success as well. So . . .

FIND AN ENGAGING, SHORT MULTIMEDIA CLIP RELATED TO YOUR INFORMATIONAL TEXT

When we are building an informational text unit, this is often the fun payoff for our hard work. Thanks to the Internet, countless video clips are readily available, and among the millions of cat videos (which Susan enjoys), it's easy to find an engaging, relevant video or audio clip related to your informational text topic without a lengthy search. The hardest part is often deciding which one to use.

For the Gorman fruit fly piece, our work was already done for us, as the article itself appears on the *New York Times* website accompanied by a short, fun video (2014) that features clips of fruit flies fighting and a voiceover that summarizes the key points of the article. Given the audiovisual nature of today's media-consuming culture, most traditionally print-oriented publications are producing online videos alongside written articles or as standalone features in their own right.

When we were working on *Using Informational Text to Teach To Kill a Mockingbird* (2014), we were delighted to find a very dated educational short film by the American Veterinary Medical Association (1982) on YouTube. Complete with ominous music and scenes of an empty playground after an attack by a rabid dog, the clip was perfect to begin our discussion of an informational text on rabies in connection with the chapter of the novel in which a rabid dog threatens Maycomb. (See www.usinginformationaltext.org for this sample unit.)

For our book on *A Raisin in the Sun* (2016), we found a wealth of videos on housing discrimination, including a funny but effective PSA (Leadership Conference on Civil and Human Rights 2008) in which a man inquires by phone about a property using different names and accents.

If your school's Internet filters prohibit access to online video sites, you can use websites like KeepVid or other browser plugins to download the video to your computer ahead of time. Taking this step is a good idea in any case, in order to remove the possibility that your fickle Internet connection might cause any playback delays during class.

You can also use sites like TubeChop, as well as video-editing software, to excerpt particular clips of a longer video, so that you just have the bits that you want to show. This is particularly important because your media clip is your opening and you don't want watching and discussing the clip to consume too much of your valuable class time. Shorter clips are always more effective!

SUPPORTING STUDENTS' MULTIMEDIA LITERACY

By starting our informational text lesson or unit with a video or audio clip, we can hook our students' interest and both activate and augment their background knowledge quickly and easily before we begin our pre-reading vocabulary work.

However, no matter how fun and light your multimedia clip might be, don't assume that your students will automatically understand all of the nuances you are using it to convey. Students are generally used to consuming video and audio fairly passively. You may need to play the clip more than once and prompt students to notice and discuss key elements during different viewings, just as you will do with your written informational text.

Susan uses a short ESPN clip (2014) about athletes using the N-word to inaugurate discussion among her sophomores about the epithet's use in *Huckleberry Finn*. Though this is a media source that many of her students are familiar with, there are so many ideas and viewpoints articulated very quickly during the clip that it always takes multiple viewings for the students to unpack the different arguments.

But it's time well spent. Reading and interpreting multimedia texts is a literacy skill as well, and one we need to support our students in developing, as the CCSS indicate (2010, 35). Remember that the PARCC and Smarter Balanced assessments will ask students to work with all kinds of texts. To give them practice with the kinds of questions they might encounter, you may want to include one or more items related to the audio or video clip in your check-for-understanding questions.

Textbox 10.1

CCSS.ELA-LITERACY.R.7: Integrate and evaluate content presented in diverse formats and media, including visually and quantitatively, as well as in words.

If your collaboration with a colleague from another discipline allows you the time for each of you to show the same video clip, go for it! Your students will be fascinated by the different ways in which you approach the media text, based on your respective instructional goals and/or disciplinary concerns, just as they will be with the informational text.

Obviously, both of you can/will be interested in the clip(s) as a preview of the key ideas about the study of aggression in the written informational text. But each of you may also have discipline-specific interests in relation to the video. For example, an English teacher might prompt students to analyze the tone and structure of the fruit fly video, including the use of background music. A science teacher, on the other hand, might focus more on what the images suggest about how the researchers conducted their experiments.

OTHER WAYS TO HOOK STUDENTS' INTEREST

Just as we might start our lesson with a video or audio clip or photograph to engage our spatial/visual and auditory learners, we can also hook their interest kinesthetically and interpersonally by presenting students with a scenario to act out, similar to the vocabulary skits.

With the fruit flies, for example, we might ask the students to simulate the behavior of different pairs of fruit flies: male pairs, female pairs, male pairs with silenced tachykinin-producing neurons, male pairs with active tachykinin-producing neurons. Of course, we don't want any actual fighting in the classroom, so perhaps the students would hold up signs representing the different kinds of fight club moves the scientists identified: the lunge, the sneak attack, tussling.

Engaging hooks can also be a place for easy, rewarding collaboration. The Gorman fruit fly article includes little information about how the scientists actually recorded their data for the study. But a science or math teacher could easily work through this question as a graphing or statistics problem.

Table 10.1 Analyze this Data and Draw Conclusions

	Aggression at Temperature 60	Aggression at Temperature 70	Aggression at Temperature 80	Aggression at Temperature 90
Fruit Flies Line 1	10%	10%	10%	11%
Fruit Flies Line 2	15%	15%	17%	15%
Fruit Flies Line 3	10%	11%	80%	80%
Fruit Flies Line 4	25%	30%	25%	30%

Perhaps the science teacher creates and supplies a table of data, as above (see Table 10.1), and asks the students to analyze the data and draw conclusions about what it might mean. Here, for example, the students might notice that fruit flies line 3 has a markedly different percentage of fruit flies recorded as aggressive at a temperature of 80 or 90 degrees. Why?

Textbox 10.2

> **CCSS.ELA-LITERACY.RST.9-10.7:** Translate quantitative or technical information expressed in words in a text into visual form (e.g., a table or chart) and translate information expressed visually or mathematically (e.g., in an equation) into words.

Or perhaps the math teacher asks the students to transform this chart into a graph or gives them a word problem to solve based on the data.

These quick, easy activities relate to and reinforce the math teacher's content, while setting the students up for a more successful reading of the numbers included in the informational text in their other class. And an activity like this might engage our logically/mathematically oriented students in the informational text as well.

In addition to appealing to our students' various learning styles, giving all of our students the opportunity to see and interpret concepts represented in different ways helps them understand the ideas more deeply and enhances their disciplinary and general literacy skills overall.

In the multimedia-based twenty-first century, our students need to develop competency in interpreting, evaluating, and expressing ideas in a wide variety of representational modes—and in translating ideas and information from one representational mode into another—in order to be successful in college, career, and their everyday lives (Wilson and Chavez 2014; Common Core Standards Initiative 2010, 62).

REFERENCES

American Veterinary Medical Association. 1982. *Rabies*. YouTube video, 12:40. Posted by "Video Archaeology2", April 4, 2011. Accessed June 12, 2013. https://www.youtube.com/watch?v=GHjJ3B2jO30.

Common Core State Standards Initiative. 2010. Common Core State Standards for English Language Arts and Literacy in History/Social Studies, Science, and Technical Subjects. Washington, DC.

Fisch, Audrey, and Susan Chenelle. 2014. *Using Informational Text to Teach To Kill a Mockingbird*. Lanham, Md.: Rowman & Littlefield.

Fisch, Audrey, and Susan Chenelle. 2016. *Using Informational Text to Teach A Raisin in the Sun*. Lanham, Md.: Rowman & Littlefield.

Gorman, James. 2014. "To Study Aggression: A Fight Club for Flies." *The New York Times*, February 3. http://www.nytimes.com/2014/02/04/science/to-study-aggression-a-fight-club-for-flies.html.

Hoopfer, Eric, Kenta Asahina, and David J. Anderson. 2014. *Science Take: Fight Club for Flies. The New York Times* video, 1:33. Posted February 3, 2014. Accessed February 4. http://www.nytimes.com/video/science/100000002686543/sciencetake-fight-club-for-flies.html.

Leadership Conference on Civil and Human Rights. 2008. *Housing discrimination – PSA*. YouTube video, 1:00. Posted by "PixorShens", June 11, 2008. Accessed February 22, 2015. https://www.youtube.com/watch?v=c_3mSW8XUZI.

Le Batard, Dan, and Bomani Jones. 2014. *Should the NFL Penalize the N-Word?* YouTube video, 1:30. Posted by "Highly Questionable on ESPN", February 24, 2014. Accessed March 14, 2014. https://www.youtube.com/watch?v=Y4Xl2Ug_ZEA.

Partnership for Assessment of Readiness for College and Careers. n.d. "Take the Test: A Different Kind of Test." Accessed July 15, 2015. http://www.parcconline.org/take-the-test/a-different-kind-of-test.

Smarter Balanced Assessment Consortium. 2012. "Performance Tasks for English Language Arts." Accessed July 15, 2015. http://www.smarterbalanced.org/wordpress/wp-content/uploads/2012/item-writing-and-review/ppt/Performance-Tasks-for-English-Language-Arts.pptx.

Wilson, Amy Alexandra, and Kathryn J. Chavez. 2014. *Reading and Representing Across the Content Areas: A Classroom Guide*. New York: Teachers College Press.

Chapter 11

Alignment with Common Core Assessments

Our model was inspired by the Common Core, not just to meet its mandates, but also to capitalize on the rich learning opportunities we think the standards can foster. And, as we noted in chapter 7, given the reality of standardized assessments in our schools today, we think it's important to give our students explicit practice in the types of performance tasks and questions they will face on the Common Core–aligned tests. Each step of our model for using informational text across disciplines does just that.

THE BEST KIND OF TEST PREPARATION

In this section, we will briefly outline how our model aligns with the CCSS assessments, so that you will be well armed to answer any questions about your test-preparation efforts. You will be able to show that you are not only thoroughly preparing your students for the assessments but also doing so in the best way possible—by embedding test preparation authentically and seamlessly into your existing curriculum. You'll even be able to say that you are going above and beyond what the assessments currently ask of students, but more on that in a moment.

First, the essential element of our model—putting texts into dialogue—is one of the biggest challenges of the PARCC and Smarter Balanced assessments, and a task that students have not always been given sufficient opportunity to practice and master, particularly in terms of putting different kinds of texts into dialogue and making a thoughtful argument.

Second, the extensive vocabulary practice activities and check-for-understanding questions are precisely modeled on the types of questions students will see on the PARCC and Smarter Balanced tests. Below we also offer organizers for planning and giving students practice with the kinds of drag-and-drop questions they might see on the assessments.

Third, the guided reading questions we offer in our model give students the opportunity to practice and develop confidence in tackling a wide variety of complex text types as active, thoughtful readers. And our emphasis on collaboration across disciplines helps students develop the disciplinary literacy skills they will need to make insightful, cogent arguments using evidence from the social studies- and science-based informational texts they will see on the PARCC and Smarter Balanced assessments.

Finally, the writing and discussion activities we advocate not only prepare students for the PARCC and Smarter Balanced performance tasks but also challenge them to go above and beyond what the tests currently ask of them.

Current samples from PARCC and Smarter Balanced only put informational texts into dialogue with other informational texts, and usually informational texts within the same discipline though they may be different types of texts.

Our model is different because it asks the student to put the informational text into dialogue with content-area knowledge and other texts, including literary texts, in order to make those rewarding cross-disciplinary connections we have discussed in this volume. Clearly, we will all have to keep thinking about how best to use these questions to prepare students for PARCC/SB while also getting them to write and think in ways that we think are important for their growth as future scholars, workers, and citizens.

PROMPTS MODELED ON THE PARCC AND SMARTER BALANCED WRITING TASKS

Below are some basic prompts that more closely align with the current standardized assessments. These can be useful as a rudimentary starting point for student writing in relation to the informational texts.

- Write an essay analyzing the arguments of X. Base the analysis on the specifics, arguments, and principles put forth in the three sources. Consider at least two of the sources.
- You have studied three sources on X. Write an essay in which you explore X. Consider how the different authors present/represent X.
- Write an essay that contrasts the primary arguments in each text about X. Think about how each author supported his/her claim with reasoning and/or evidence.
- Write an essay comparing the information presented in each text. Use evidence.

- Write a multi-paragraph argumentative/persuasive essay/statement in which you take a position on the issue of X. You will present your statement to audience Y. Use evidence from the sources you have read to support your argument.

We also offer the T-chart organizer that follows to guide your students' reading and thinking in preparation for these general prompts.

Note, however, that we strongly encourage teachers to develop more challenging and engaging writing prompts. Remember, the more mundane and less interesting task is often more difficult and less successful; when we ask our students to do more, they so often rise to the challenge.

By using our model, you can thoroughly prepare your students for CCSS-aligned and other standardized assessments while pursuing rich, authentic learning within your discipline and across disciplines, instead of having to drop your content and curriculum in order to undertake the disconnected test-prep activities that we know are so disruptive to students' learning.

ORGANIZER FOR READING INFORMATIONAL TEXTS IN DIALOGUE

You can prepare your students for the writing prompts on the PARCC/SB assessments by having them use or make their own T-chart organizer like the one below. Depending on the prompt or your instructional focus, students can take notes that help them compare the speakers, occasions, purpose, tone, emphasis, key arguments and evidence, or structure of two related texts (Table 11.1).

Table 11.1 T-chart Organizer

TEXT #1	TEXT #2

MATCHING ARGUMENTS WITH EVIDENCE OR COUNTERARGUMENTS

DRAG-and-DROP QUESTIONS: The CCSS assessments feature questions in which students must arrange excerpts of texts to match specific arguments with their evidence or counterarguments. You can use these organizers to plan drag-and-drop questions if you have access to such technology or to give your students practice with similar tasks on paper. (Editable versions of these organizers are available at www.usinginformationaltext.org.)

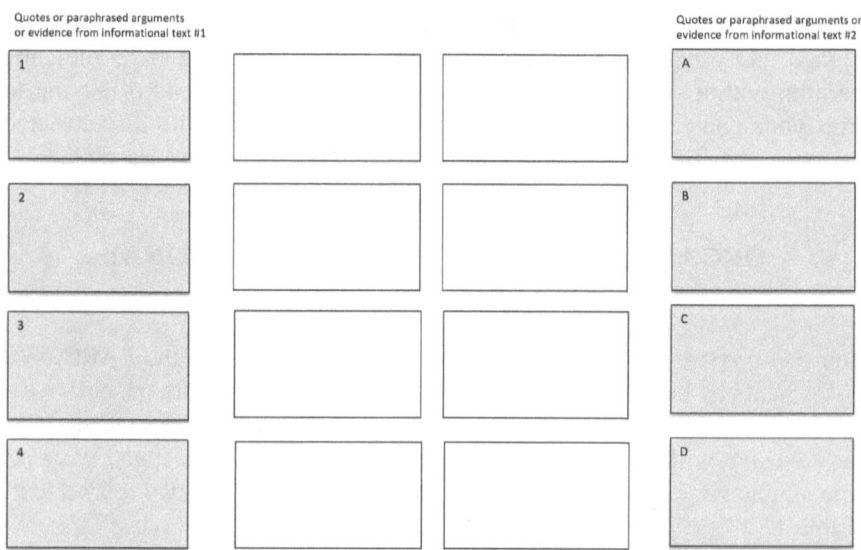

Figure 11.1   Matching Arguments with Evidence or Counter Arguments

PUTTING ELEMENTS IN SEQUENTIAL ORDER: The CCSS assessments feature questions in which students put elements described in the text in sequential order (e.g., steps in an experiment). You can use these organizers to plan drag-and-drop questions if you have access to such technology or to give your students practice with similar tasks on paper (Figure 11.2).

Alignment with Common Core Assessments 81

Quotes or paraphrased arguments or evidence from informational text #1	Place the arguments or evidence from the left-hand column in order below
A	1
B	2
C	3
D	4

Figure 11.2 Putting Elements in Sequential Order

Chapter 12

You Can Do This

Keys to Implementation

THE POWER OF SMALL-SCALE COLLABORATIONS

So, you've found a good-natured colleague with whom to work and you've identified a key topic or content-area concept about which you plan to collaborate. You've found an informational text that the two of you find engaging, both on its own as an interesting piece of complex text and in terms of how you hope it will allow you to engage your students with your key topic or content-area concept.

From this point forward, every collaboration will be somewhat different. And that's very much okay.

In chapter 2, we discussed Kate Cronk and Hallie Edgerly's (2015) collaboration at Adel DeSoto Minburn Community School District in Adel, Iowa, in which they completely integrated their language arts/science class for a cross-disciplinary unit centered around invention. Their work was impressive.

But this kind of wholesale interconnectedness may not be possible in your school. In fact, we think it's highly improbable to imagine this kind of integrated collaboration at the high school level.

Even after you've found a collaborative and collegial colleague with whom you can work, the hurdles to collaboration still exist.

You and your colleague may not have schedules that allow for co-teaching or common planning time.

In the ideal universe, you would share entirely the same group of students, but perhaps you don't. Perhaps you have only some overlapping students, or perhaps your colleague taught these students in 9th grade and you now have them in 10th grade.

That's okay.

Textbox 12.1 Steps to Collaboration

- Find a collegial colleague with whom to collaborate
- Find an engaging informational text and hook or multimedia clip that connects your respective content areas
- Cut! Use excerpts
- Front-load key vocabulary words (not too many!) and concepts
- Use sidebar reading prompts to promote active reading
- Use multiple-choice questions informally to check for understanding and practice test-taking skills
- Use open-ended questions to extend thinking and develop literacy skills across the disciplines
- Close with a class activity that gives students opportunities to use content-area knowledge for authentic purposes

As we said earlier, don't underestimate the power of small-scale collaborations. These can:

1. be doable;
2. substantially increase students' cross-disciplinary literacy skills;
3. help students see the ways in which different disciplines are not isolated silos;
4. help students see the ways in which different disciplines ask different questions about texts, think about evidence differently, and construct arguments differently; and
5. make students feel smart because they already know things from one classroom when they enter another.

So, given the fact that you probably aren't going to end up standing together in each other's rooms for two weeks teaching about neuroscience, aggression, and *Lord of the Flies* to an entirely shared group of students, how are you going to make this work?

DIFFERENT COLLABORATIVE CONFIGURATIONS

Because each pair of teachers and configuration of students is going to be slightly different, what we are going to outline below isn't going to work exactly the same way for every group. But read through these ideas and think about how to make them work for you.

First of all, think about how you are going to divide up the teaching of your informational text. Again, there's no one approach and no right way to go about this.

1. Very Limited Integration

In scenario one, the science teacher might be unwilling/unable to give up any class time at all for the unit. Still, he/she is willing to collaborate, but only the language arts teacher will work with the article in class.

So, the two teachers sit together to plan. They discuss the various scientific concepts and topics at play in the Gorman article with which the students should be familiar. They talk about cutting the informational text so as to preserve the information related to these concepts in a way that allows the article to remain meaningful in relation to the key science issues. They work together on crafting discussion and writing prompts that allow students to make use of their science content knowledge while also satisfying the needs of the language arts teacher. The science teacher might agree to show the video clip and briefly discuss its key points in class to preview what the students will see in their English class.

Perhaps the science teacher is able to get coverage for his/her class in order to attend the students' end-of-unit presentations or perhaps the language arts teacher decides to forgo the end-of-unit project because he or she is working largely alone.

2. Logistical Issues But More Integration

In scenario two, the science teacher and the language arts teacher are both willing and able to devote class time to the Gorman article. They have time to plan and want to collaborate. But they share some but not all of the same students!

As difficult as their scenario might sound, this can be a particularly fruitful collaboration.

These two teachers can both teach the unit. Vocabulary activities and check-for-understanding questions can be conducted as homework but reviewed in class, which will mean some extra review for some of the students (never a tragedy). Vocabulary skits can be conducted in both classes, for even more fun and more "massive practice" (Moffett and Wagner 1991, 10). Reading of the text might be conducted as a whole-class activity in one class; in the next, students who have already read the text in one class might serve as peer discussion leaders, guiding their other peers in group reading.

Teachers might diverge in their discussion and writing questions and class activities, choosing to select tasks most suited to their content-area concerns. Students might select groups for their activities based on whether or not they are shared students.

Again, class activity presentations might or might not occur during class time, with both teachers present, or after school. For shared students, the teachers might even decide to use a shared assessment tool and to collaborate in the grading.

3. Near-Total Integration

In scenario three, the science teacher might agree to take on in full the teaching of Gorman's fruit fly article, leaving the language arts teacher to share in as many or as few activities as he/she might like. In this case, the language arts teacher might work with the same media clip in her class, engaging the students, as we noted in chapter 10, in a comparison of the kinds of disciplinary-specific questions we might pose about a media clip in a language arts class and encouraging students to think about, in contrast, how their discussion of this same clip in science involved different types of questions and foci.

The science teacher might do the pre-reading vocabulary work in science class, with the language arts teacher supporting the endeavor by reinforcing any particularly difficult words. The science teacher might work through the informational text in class, while the language arts teacher might take on the check-for-understanding questions. The science teacher might use a science-oriented discussion and writing prompt, while the language arts teacher might ask the students to write about fruit fly aggression in relation to *Lord of the Flies*.

Perhaps the students and both teachers would come together either during or after school for a presentation of the students' summative activity based on the unit.

DON'T DESPAIR—WHATEVER SCENARIO YOU FIND YOURSELF IN

The permutations are endless. We don't need to tell you that where there's a will, there's a way. If you are motivated to collaborate with a colleague on an informational text in order to further your students' cross-disciplinary literacy and enhance their engagement with the content areas, you can make it happen.

CAUTIONS

Here are some tips based on what we've learned from doing these units with students.

1. Don't skip the vocabulary

You may think you don't have enough time to do the vocabulary activities, and you're tempted to skip ahead to the reading. First of all, remember that you can do the vocabulary exercises quickly. Assign sets of questions to groups and have the groups do the work and report back to the class.

This allows all students to gain some familiarity with the words, produces experts on the words (in the groups) who can be called upon during the reading to offer assistance, and moves things along in terms of time. And once your students get used to this kind of work, particularly in terms of dictionary work, they will gain skill and speed. Vocabulary can be such a challenge and can be the single stumbling block that makes a student feel dumb and turns him off of a reading.

2. Use your media to hook your students

Whether you begin with a short media clip, a provocative graphic or infographic, a political cartoon, or an intriguing picture, work to your students' strengths by focusing their attention first on a text that is more accessible. At the same time, don't forget that all texts require thoughtful, careful analysis, and while your students may think they are savvy media viewers (and they may be), you may want to play and work through your media clip more than once.

Also, you may choose to decide whether or not you want to use your multimedia hook as your opening based on the difficulty of its content and vocabulary. If your hook requires some fundamental understanding of key concepts and vocabulary, do your vocabulary work first. If your students can manage, begin with the multimedia.

3. Take your time working your way through the text

Use your sidebar questions to differentiate instruction. Allow students to work on some of these in pairs or groups and then come to whole-class discussion. And don't forget to talk with them about how the sidebar questions work. Try to make explicit for them the fact that these are the types of questions a good reader needs to be asking as he/she is working with complex text.

4. Take time with the check-for-understanding questions

Use these thoughtfully as teaching tools rather than high-stakes assessments. Notice the ways in which your students get tripped up by the question formats even when they have the understanding of the ideas. These are your teachable moments to impart some of the test-taking strategies that can benefit your students for years to come.

As your students get more comfortable, have them, in groups or for homework, create some of their own check-for-understanding questions that you can then use for informal assessment. This will lighten your workload (although don't expect their questions to be perfect), allow them to both demonstrate their understanding of the text and practice the format of multiple-choice questions (nothing teaches you as much about how to attack multiple-choice questions than making up your own wrong answers), and finally give your students some sense of ownership over the larger standardized testing world in which they generally are powerless.

5. **Use the discussion and writing questions and class activities as much or as little as your time allows**

   Not having two weeks to set aside to devote to a drawn-out discussion of aggression in *Lord of the Flies* doesn't mean you can't take a day or two to talk about aggression in male fruit flies. Even if you take a different focus with the text, don't underestimate the power of bringing in a different avenue of understanding for your students. Hook that science kid in the back of the room with the fruit fly neurons, and he may surprise you with how engaged he remains for the rest of the discussion of the novel!

HOW LONG WILL THIS TAKE?

We think you can do a solid job with a properly prepared and nicely excerpted informational text in two short class periods (42 minutes or so). This estimate includes the basics: group work in class on vocabulary, a viewing (or two) and discussion of some kind of multimedia clip, and reading and discussion as a class (with some group breakout discussions) of the text itself.

Carefully discussing and working through multiple-choice questions will take longer, as will your substantive discussion and writing questions and class activities. So maybe you do these sometimes but not always.

HOW OFTEN SHOULD I DO THIS?

Don't let your desire for perfection and complete control force you to sacrifice the good for the perfect.

You should do this often.

Why? Because we want our students to be doing this work—making connections across the disciplines, reading all sorts of complex texts, and building their confidence and skills as readers and thinkers.

So, reach out to that friendly new math teacher who looks like he's up for a challenge. Identify an existing unit to build a collaboration around, or think about a moment in the school year (the first day, Halloween, the day before break) where you have a little flexibility and time. And give this a try.

If you regularly integrate short informational texts into your classroom, your students will start coming to you with connections of their own—whether in terms of cross-disciplinary links they have identified in their own classes or in terms of text connections they have found on their own. They may just surprise you with what they can come up with as empowered intellectuals-in-training.

CELEBRATE YOUR ACCOMPLISHMENTS AND ASK FOR TIME TO DO THIS WORK

Finally, we would be remiss if we did not cajole you to speak up about your collaborative successes.

It's not easy to be a teacher today. And it can be even more challenging to be that teacher who thinks outside the box.

In your local community, talk to your administrators about your collaborative experiments and accomplishments. Invite colleagues, parents, and administrators to celebrate your students' presentations.

In the broader professional world, share your accomplishments with your peers. Present at a local or national conference. Be that inspiring team of teachers who shares how their small collaboration was able to be transformative. Write about your work for your state or national professional journal.

And ask for time from your administrators to do this work. This kind of collaboration is so full of potential because when we have the time to use our colleagues as "resources for learning," we can develop our schools into "communities of practice" in which teachers come together to "support students as they learn to explore the multiple literacies of the disciplines" (NCTE 3). We need, however, the time to put our heads together to have conversations about what our students are learning, what our struggles are, and how we can work together.

What we've tried to offer here is an easy-to-use template with straightforward, step-by-step directions. You've bought this book and read through to the end. You have the tools you need. You are ready to reach out to a peer teacher and make this work. Start with our model or modify it to make it your own.

If you master the ability to integrate an informational text successfully into your existing curriculum, you will be empowered to help your students see the connections between what they are learning in their different classes and the bigger issues in the world at large.

As Mills and Moon (2014) write, "we value that CCSS also provides an opportunity for teachers to creatively address students' future needs by connecting content-area skills to the real world" (91). Hear, hear.

We also value that the Common Core and particularly the emphasis it places on cross-disciplinary literacy and collaboration restore teachers to their place as intellectual leaders in the classroom.

REFERENCES

Cronk, Kate, and Hallie Edgerly. 2015. "Collaboration that Works: Science, Literacy, and 21st Century Skills." Lecture presented at the annual conference for ASCD, Houston, Texas: March 21–23.

Mills, Allisyn, and Seungho Moon. 2014. Teaching Equity through *Gatsby* in the Age of CCSS. *English Journal*, 104.2, 86–92.

Moffett, James, and Betty J. Wagner. 1991. *Student-Centered Language Arts, K-12*. New York: Heinemann.

National Council of Teachers of English (NCTE). 2011. *Literacies of Disciplines: A Policy Research Brief Produced by the National Council of Teachers of English*. Accessed June 15, 2015. http://www.ncte.org/library/NCTEFiles/Resources/Journals/CC/0211-sep2011/CC0211Policy.pdf.

Appendix A

The Fruit Fly Unit

The issue of male aggression is central to all of Lord of the Flies, *but this passage (or a slightly longer excerpt up to "Jack stood up, holding out his hands") from early in the novel sets up the issue of male aggression well.*

EXCERPT FROM THE *LORD OF THE FLIES*

Fifteen yards from the drove Jack stopped, and his arm, straightening, pointed at the sow. He looked round in inquiry to make sure that everyone understood and the other boys nodded at him. The row of right arms slid back.

"Now!"

The drove of pigs started up; and at a range of only ten yards the wooden spears with fire-hardened points flew toward the chosen pig. One piglet, with a demented shriek, rushed into the sea trailing Roger's spear behind it. The sow gave a gasping squeal and staggered up, with two spears sticking in.

Before the others could examine the drop of blood, Jack had swerved off, judging a trace, touching a bough that gave. So he followed, mysteriously right and assured, and the hunters trod behind him.

He stopped before a covert.

"In there."

They surrounded the covert but the sow got away with the sting of another spear in her flank. The trailing butts hindered her and the sharp, cross-cut points were a torment. She blundered into a tree, forcing a spear still deeper; and after that any of the hunters could follow her easily by the drops of vivid blood. The afternoon wore on, hazy and dreadful with damp heat; the sow staggered her way ahead of them, bleeding and mad, and the hunters followed, wedded to her in lust, excited by the long chase and the dropped blood.

Golding, William. *Lord of the Flies*. New York: Perigree Books, 2003, 134–135. Print.

PRE-READING VOCABULARY ACTIVITIES

Key vocabulary for "To Study Aggression":
neuroscientist
tussles
neurons
hypothesis
genetically modified
suppresses

Types of vocabulary activities:

A. *Use context clues*: Read the following sentences and use context clues to determine the meaning of the italicized words.

1. The research began with a *hypothesis* about what causes aggression. The scientists tested their theory with experiments. Based on the context, what is a scientific *hypothesis*? Why do scientists need to test a *hypothesis* with experiments?

B. *More context clues*: Here your task is to use context clues to understand the meaning of the italicized word or phrase.

2. The researchers tested *genetically modified* fruit flies that had been engineered so that their neurons would react to a certain temperature in the environment. *Genetically modified* here means

   a. aggressive
   b. reactive
   c. scientifically altered
   d. professionally trained

3. Which word from the sentence above best helps the reader understand the meaning of *genetically modified*?

   a. engineered
   b. react
   c. researchers
   d. environment

Appendix A 93

C. *Use the dictionary* to look up the italicized words and answer the following questions based on their definitions.

    4. If someone wants to be a *neuroscientist*, that person is most likely interested in what? Why do you think someone might become interested in neuroscience?

    5. Some people argue that the *neurons* in teenagers' brains don't always work the way they should. Why would someone say that? Do you think your *neurons* work well? Why or why not?

D. *Use the dictionary in order to understand the uncommon meaning of this common word.*

    6. Gorman writes that, "When these neurons were silenced, the researchers were able to decrease aggression." These neurons weren't shushed or kept from making noise. What does silenced mean in this instance? How do you think neurons can be silenced?

E. *Practice using the word correctly* by choosing the correct form of the word that best fits in the blank within the following sentences.

    7. The principal has _____ that if students are well fed, they will do better on their schoolwork. He plans to test his _____ by offering good breakfasts to all students.

       a. hypothesis ... hypothesize
       b. hypothesized ... hypothesis
       c. hypothesized ... hypothesize
       d. hypothesis ... hypothesization

F. *Vocabulary skits*

Use the model sentences and definitions to understand the words in question. Create a skit in which you address the given topic. Every member of the group must use the vocabulary word at least once during your performance of the skit.

    8. *tussle*—to have a fight; a fight, brawl, scuffle

- I think men are more likely to get into *tussles* than women.
- My father always wants to *tussle* with me about my chores, but I am doing the best I can.
- The endless *tussles* in Congress would be amusing if they didn't have such important implications for our future.

Scenario: Create a skit in which a group of scientists discuss the relationship between gender and aggression. Are men naturally more aggressive than women? Are women less likely to get into *tussles* than men? (Feel free to have the scientists get into a verbal (but not physical) *tussle* during their conversation.)

TO STUDY AGGRESSION, A FIGHT CLUB FOR FLIES

By JAMES GORMAN

The New York Times

FEB. 3, 2014

> **Reflect** on the title. What do you think the article will be about? Have you ever heard of a fight club? Would you expect flies to have a fight club?
>
> **Reflect** on the kind of informational text. Where and when was this article published? What does that tell you? What do you think the purpose of the article is? How reliable do you think the information is?

Males' aggression toward each other is an old story throughout the animal kingdom. It's not that females aren't aggressive, but in many species, male-on-male battles are more common.

Take fruit flies. "The males are more aggressive than females," said David J. Anderson, a California Institute of Technology *neuroscientist* who knows their *tussles* well. Dr. Anderson runs a kind of fight club for fruit flies in his lab at Caltech, with the goal of understanding the deep evolutionary roots of very fundamental behaviors.

> **Vocabulary:** If David Anderson is a neuroscientist, what does he study? Given the fact that the paragraph discusses fruit flies, what else can you tell about Dr. Anderson's research?
>
> **Vocabulary:** The article suggests that Anderson "knows their tussles well." Put this into your own words. Who is tussling here? What does it mean for Anderson to "know their tussles"?

Dr. Anderson, Kenta Asahina, and a group of their colleagues recently identified one gene and a tiny group of *neurons,* sometimes as few as three, present only in the brains of male fruit flies, that can control aggression.

> **Key Idea:** The article indicates that Anderson and his colleagues identified "a tiny group of neurons . . . that can control aggression." What is the idea here? Why would scientists be interested in studying aggression? Why would they care that a small group of neurons control aggression?

The gene is also found in mammals, and has also been associated with aggression in some mammalian species, perhaps even in humans, although that is not clear.

The discovery, reported in the journal *Cell* last month, does not tell the whole story of fly aggression. Some fighting is inextricably linked to food and mating, while the mechanism the scientists found is not. But it is a striking indication of how brain structure and chemistry work together, as well as a reminder that as different as humans and flies are, they are not always very far apart (see Figure A.1).

> **Reflect** on the picture and caption. What information is offered here? Why do you think the author included this particular photo?

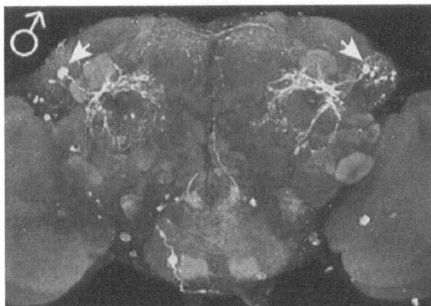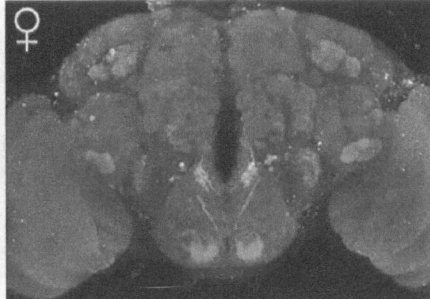

Figure A.1 At Caltech, researchers identified a gene and a tiny group of neurons in male flies that control aggression. Left, a male fruit fly's brain. The arrows point to the neurons that the female brain lacks. Photo: Kenta Asahina

The research began, Dr. Anderson said, with the *hypothesis* that neuropeptides, which are a kind of hormone in the brain, had a role in controlling aggression.

To find out which neuropeptides were important, the team tested different lines, of *genetically modified* fruit flies. All lines had been engineered so that at a certain temperature, around 80 degrees, a chemical change would make specific neurons fire. In each line the neurons were different. They tested about 40 lines of flies, raising the temperature to increase the firing of neurons and determine which flies showed increased aggressive behavior. They used another technique to make neurons they were studying become fluorescent green so they could see their anatomy and location. And using a variety of tools, they narrowed the search to neurons that were producing the neuropeptide tachykinin. When they compared the brains of male and female flies, they found a few neurons, present only in the male, that produced tachykinin. When these neurons were silenced, the researchers were able to decrease aggression. The emergence of tachykinin was very interesting because mammals have several different kinds of tachykinin, including substance P, which has been connected

Key Idea: The writer of this article suggests that "as different as humans and flies are, they are not always very far apart." Why does he say this? Why is he making this point in an article about fruit flies?

Key Idea: The research began with "the hypothesis that neuropeptides, which are a kind of hormone in the brain, had a role in controlling aggression. Put this into your own words. What was the hypothesis for the research?

Key Idea: How did the scientists use genetic modifications in their experiments? What did they discover? What is tachykinin and why is it important?

Key Idea: The article explains that substance P is a kind of tachykinin. Why is that important? Do fruit flies have substance P? Who has substance P? What do scientists think about substance P?

to aggression in rodents and has a variety of suspected roles in human beings, including a possible link to aggression.

They now had identified a cluster of neurons, as few as three, that caused an increase in aggression. Those few neurons were only in males. They were active when males were fighting each other. The researchers did more genetic manipulation, deleting and adding copies of tachykinin genes, so that the neurons would produce more or less of the chemical. They found that with enough tachykinin produced by these few neurons, flies became more or less aggressive. They could even make small flies attack bigger flies.

In the end, they clearly established that a significant behavioral difference in male and female flies was based in the brain. What this might mean for humans is unclear. A drug that *suppresses* the activity of substance P in humans had, at one time, seemed very promising as an antidepressant. It failed in clinical trials, but Dr. Anderson and his co-authors suggested in the *Cell* paper that it might be tested for symptoms like uncontrollable anger that can affect people with illnesses like post-traumatic stress syndrome.

Notice that the article suggests that "What this might mean for humans is unclear." What does this sentence mean? What claims are the scientists making about aggression in fruit flies? Can they make any claims, based on the research, about aggression in humans?

It is clear that humans and flies have more in common than it might appear. Dr. Anderson said, "Studying aggression in fruit flies can actually teach us something about some of the molecules that control aggression."

Key Idea: What does the article suggest we can learn from studying aggression in fruit flies?

CHECK FOR UNDERSTANDING

1. In "To Study Aggression," James Gorman explains that "All lines had been engineered so that at a certain temperature, around 80 degrees, a chemical change would make specific neurons fire . . . they narrowed the search to neurons that were producing the neuropeptide tachykinin." By "fire," Gorman here means

   a. explode
   b. combust
   c. produce tachykinin
   d. become very hot

2. Which word(s) from the sentence above best help(s) the reader understand the meaning of "fire" in this context?

a. 80 degrees
b. certain temperature
c. producing the neuropeptide
d. engineered

3. Which of the following sentences best states the main idea of "To Study Aggression"?
   a. Men are more aggressive than women.
   b. The brains of fruit flies are like the brains of mammals.
   c. Studying aggression in male fruit flies may help us understand aggression in humans.
   d. Substance P seems to be the key to understanding aggression.

4. Select the THREE pieces of evidence from the article that BEST support your answer to question 3.
   a. "They could even make small flies attack bigger flies."
   b. "A drug that suppresses the activity of substance P in humans had, at one time, seemed very promising as an antidepressant."
   c. "Studying aggression in fruit flies can actually teach us something about some of the molecules that control aggression."
   d. "It is clear that humans and flies have more in common than it might appear."
   e. "The research began, Dr. Anderson said, with the hypothesis that neuropeptides, which are a kind of hormone in the brain, had a role in controlling aggression."
   f. "When they compared the brains of male and female flies, they found a few neurons, present only in the male, that produced tachykinin."
   g. "But it is a striking indication of how brain structure and chemistry work together, as well as a reminder that as different as humans and flies are, they are not always very far apart."
   h. "Males' aggression toward each other is an old story."

5. James Gorman begins his article with the statement that "Males' aggression toward each other is an old story throughout the animal kingdom." Which paraphrase best explains the writer's thinking here?
   a. People have long believed that men are more aggressive than women.
   b. People have long believed that males are more aggressive than females.
   c. Males are more aggressive toward animals.
   d. While many people think males are more aggressive than females, that's actually just a story.

6. Which question is unanswered by the reading?

   a. Why are men more aggressive than women?
   b. What role do neuropeptides have in relationship to aggression?
   c. What makes male fruit flies more aggressive than female fruit flies?
   d. What kind of behavior is linked with substance P?

7. What is the function of the illustration in the article?

   a. to make the article easier to read
   b. to offer a visual illustration of the difference between male and female fruit fly brains
   c. to explain male aggression
   d. to show how similar male and female fruit fly brains are

WRITING AND DISCUSSION

OPEN-ENDED RESPONSE #1:

James Gorman discusses research on aggression in fruit flies by a group of scientists.

- Why, according to Gorman, are the scientists interested in aggression in fruit flies?
- What have these scientists discovered about aggression in fruit flies? What are the implications of their discoveries for humans? What questions remain unanswered by the research?

Use information *and textual evidence from the article* to support your response. Be sure to follow the conventions of standard English.

OPEN-ENDED RESPONSE #2:

Use what you've learned about male fruit fly aggression in James Gorman's article in relation to the excerpt (the scene in which the boys attack and kill the sow) from William Golding's *Lord of the Flies*.

- How might the scene from *Lord of the Flies* reflect the concerns about aggression in Gorman's article?
- How might the scientists Gorman discusses analyze the behavior of the boys in the scene? If they could study the boys, what might they be interested in learning more about?

- How does Gorman's discussion of male fruit fly aggression change the way you read this scene in *Lord of the Flies*. Do you find this a compelling way to think about this scene and/or the novel generally? Why or why not?

Develop your essay *by providing textual evidence from both texts.* Be sure to follow the conventions of standard English.

Open-Ended Response Rubric

(Rubric available as an editable Microsoft Word document at www.usinginformationaltext.org/downloads.)

Appendix A.2 Open-ended Response Rubric

Category	4—Excellent	3—Good	2—Satisfactory	1—Unsatisfactory
Evidence and examples (cites relevant and sufficient textual evidence)	Essay uses and discusses thoroughly a wide range of textual evidence and examples	Essay uses and discusses a wide range of textual evidence and examples although the discussion of these examples may be incomplete or uneven	Essay uses and discusses some textual evidence examples although the discussion of these examples may be incomplete or uneven	Essay uses and discusses a limited number of examples and/or textual evidence discusses these minimally
Focused and cohesive argument (valid reasoning and organization)	Essay makes a focused and cohesive argument in response to prompt	Essay makes an argument in response to prompt, but the argument may not be fully cohesive or focused throughout	Essay makes an uneven and not particularly clear argument in response prompt	Essay makes no real argument in response to prompt
Insight and understanding (determines the meaning of and analyze text)	Essay shows insight into and understanding of the text(s) and content-area knowledge	Essay shows some insight into and understanding of the text(s) and content-area knowledge	Essay shows limited insight into and understanding of the text(s) and content-area knowledge	Essay shows little insight into and understanding of the text(s) and content-area knowledge
Grammar and mechanics (conventions of standard English)	Essay contains few errors in grammar and mechanics and they do not inhibit meaning; no patterns of error	Essay contains some errors in grammar and mechanics and they do not inhibit meaning; errors do not fall into patterns	Essay contains frequent errors in grammar and mechanics that may inhibit meaning; writing exhibits some patterns of error	Essay contains numerous errors in grammar and mechanics that inhibit meaning; writing exhibits several patterns of error
Vocabulary use (uses domain-specific vocabulary)	Essay uses precise, varied, and strong vocabulary; several key vocabulary words from the unit are used correctly	Essay uses some precise, varied, and strong vocabulary; essay attempts to use key vocabulary words from the unit, but these may be used infrequently or with limited accuracy	Vocabulary choices are sometimes imprecise, repetitive, and weak; essay does not attempt to use key vocabulary words from the unit or uses these ineffectively and inaccurately	Vocabulary choices are vague, repetitive, and weak; essay does not attempt to use key vocabulary words from the unit
Documentation (in-text citation and works cited)	Essay conforms to the appropriate style guidelines (MLA) for in-text citation and works cited	Essay conforms with limited errors to the appropriate style guidelines (MLA) for in-text citation and works cited	Essay attempts to conform to the appropriate style guidelines (MLA) for in-text citation and works cited but does so ineffectively or inaccurately	Essay does not conform to the appropriate style guidelines (MLA) for in-text citation and works cited

Appendix A

CLASS ACTIVITY: TALK SHOW ON AGGRESSION IN FRUIT FLIES AND HUMANS

Task: Your goal is to conduct a TV talk show debate around the question, "Is aggression genetic?" The discussion will incorporate the viewpoints of multiple guests, including scientists, experts on aggression, and one or more characters from *Lord of the Flies*. Each student will be required to determine (based on research and/or understanding of the texts read in class) how his/her character would act and speak during the debate.

Talk show host or cohosts: Prepares questions for both panelists and audience members. Acts as moderator for the debate, asking questions of the panelists and audience members, and promoting balanced and civil discussion among all parties.

Panelists:

- James Gorman
- David J. Anderson, neuroscientist
- Piggy
- Jack
- William Golding
- Other characters from *Lord of the Flies*, as desired

Outside experts (these experts will be expected to offer evidence to back up their assertions about the origins of aggression):

- Outside experts on aggression in athletes
- Outside experts on aggression among girls
- Outside experts on cyberbullying

In addition, each student must produce the following:

1. *Explanation of character:* Write a reflective narrative in which you explain how you went about determining how your character would act, what he or she would say during the debate in response to particular questions, and how he or she would perceive and react to the other characters. Justify (with textual evidence) how your character's words and actions make sense based on your research and/or your understanding of *Lord of the Flies* and the fruit fly informational text and any additional research you might have consulted.

2. *Postdebate evaluation:* 1) Write a reflection in which you evaluate how the talk show debate was conducted. Discuss how well your classmates represented their characters: did their words and actions make sense for their roles? 2) Reflecting on the informational text readings, *Lord of the Flies*, yours and your peers' research, as well as the exchange of ideas during the debate, discuss the essential question: "Is aggression genetic?" How has your understanding of this question changed?

Class Activity Rubric

(Rubric available as an editable Microsoft Word document at www.usinginformationaltext.org/downloads.)

Appendix A.3 Class Activity Rubric

Category	4—Excellent	3—Good	2—Satisfactory	1—Unsatisfactory
Performance of role (presentation of knowledge and ideas)	Performance demonstrates strong and insightful comprehension of role through ample, effective reference to evidence from the novel, the informational text, content-area knowledge, and/or outside research	Performance demonstrates solid comprehension of role through frequent, effective reference to evidence from the novel, the informational text, content-area knowledge, and/or outside research	Performance demonstrates some comprehension of role through occasional, though perhaps vague or ineffective, reference to evidence from the novel, the informational text, content-area knowledge, and/or outside research	Performance does not demonstrate comprehension of role through reference to evidence from the novel, the informational text, content-area knowledge, and/or outside research
Collaboration (initiate and participate effectively in conversation & collaboration)	Student participates clearly and persuasively in debate	Student participates somewhat clearly and persuasively in debate	Student participates somewhat clearly but perhaps not persuasively in debate	Student does not participate clearly or persuasively in debate
Explanation of role (cite relevant and sufficient textual evidence)	Reflection demonstrates strong and insightful comprehension of role through ample, effective reference to evidence from the novel, the informational text, content-area knowledge, and/or outside research	Reflection demonstrates solid comprehension of role through frequent, effective reference to evidence from the novel, the informational text, content-area knowledge, and/or outside research	Reflection demonstrates some comprehension of role through occasional, though perhaps vague or ineffective, reference to evidence from the novel, the informational text, content-area knowledge, and/or outside research	Reflection does not demonstrate comprehension of role through reference to evidence from the novel, the informational text, content-area knowledge, and/or outside research
Evaluation and reflection (cite relevant and sufficient textual evidence)	Evaluation and reflection make clear, insightful arguments based on substantial specific evidence from debate and texts	Evaluation and reflection make clear arguments based on specific evidence from debate and texts	Evaluation and reflection make arguments that may be vague or not clearly based on evidence from debate and texts	Evaluation and reflection do not make arguments based on evidence from debate and texts
Vocabulary (use domain-specific vocabulary)	Several key vocabulary words from the unit are used correctly in debate and/or narratives	Some key vocabulary words from the unit are used correctly in debate and/or narratives	One or more key vocabulary words from the unit are used but perhaps not correctly or effectively	No key vocabulary words from the unit are used in debate and/or narratives
Documentation (in-text citation and works cited)	Essay(s) conform to the appropriate style guidelines (MLA) for in-text citation and works cited	Essay(s) conform with limited errors to the appropriate style guidelines (MLA) for in-text citation and works cited	Essay(s) attempt to conform to the appropriate style guidelines (MLA) for in-text citation and works cited but do so ineffectively or inaccurately	Essay(s) do not conform to the appropriate style guidelines (MLA) for in-text citation and works cited

Index

Adel DeSoto Minburn Community School, 13, 83
ASCD, 13, 15
The Atlantic, 1

Beck, Isabel L., 33, 39, 41
Burke, Jim, 5

Chavez, Kathryn, J., 5, 67, 75
check-for-understanding questions, 52, 86–88, 96–98
City of Chicago Commission on Human Relations, 23
class activities and projects, ix, 65–69, 85–86, 88, 100–102
Claudette Colvin, 14
CNN, 25
Common Core, vii–viii, xi, 1–3, 12, 21–22, 33, 36, 38, 51–52, 54, 63, 73, 75, 77, 90;
  anchor standard 1 for speaking and listening, *11*, 66;
  anchor standard 2 for speaking and listening, 66;
  anchor standard 3 for speaking and listening, 66;
  anchor standard 4 for language, *41*;
  anchor standard 4 for speaking and listening, 66;
  anchor standard 5 for speaking and listening, 66;
  anchor standard 6 for speaking and listening, 66;
  anchor standard 6 for writing, 66;
  anchor standard 7 for reading, *73*;
  anchor standard 7 for reading science and technical subjects, *74*;
  anchor standard 9 for reading, *7*;
  Appendix A, 2;
  cross-content literacy standards of, 1, 21–22, 90;
  informational text mandate of, xi, 2;
  introduction to, 2;
  language standard, 35
co-teaching, 14, 61, 83
craft and structure, 47, 50, 52, 55, 57
  See also multiple-choice
Cronk, Kate, 13–15, 83

differentiation, 8, 46, 68, 87
disciplines:
  math, 74–75;
  science, 23, 30–31, 61–63, 73–75
Downers Grove, IL, 12–13
drag-and-drop questions, 78, 80–81

Edgerly, Hallie, 13–15, 83

engagement, viii–ix, 34, 39–40, 43, 45–46
ESPN, 73
Esposito, Chris, 12
essential questions, 5–6, 8, 14, 65, 67, 101
evidence, use of, 46, 54, 61–62, 68
excerpts, 23, 29–31

Fisher, Douglas, 33
Francese, Lauren, 14
Freeman, Meaghan, 1–2
Frey, Nancy, 33

Golding, William, viii, 6, 9, 91–92, 98–100
Google:
 Drive, 17;
 news alerts, 24;
 search, 23
Gorman, James, 6–7, 12, 24, 40, 72, 74, 85–86, 93–98, 100
The Great Gatsby, 16, 24
guided reading questions, 16, 45–47;
 sidebar, 45–46, 49

hooks, ix, 73–74
Huckleberry Finn, 73

informational text, 55–56;
 editorial, 23, 28, 33, 45;
 government report, 23;
 interview transcript, 23;
 news report or article, 23, 28, 33, 45;
 op-ed, vii;
 primary source, 23–24;
 scientific study, 28, 30, 33, 45, 49;
 structure of, 28–29, 55;
 Supreme Court decisions, vii, 16–17, 49.
 See also multimedia texts
integration of knowledge and ideas, 52, 55, 57.
 See also multiple-choice
International Literacy Association, 4–5, 11

jigsaw, 46
Johnson, Philip, 12
Jones, Stephen, vii

KeepVid, 72
key ideas and details, 52, 54, 57.
 See also multiple-choice
Kucan, Linda, 33, 39, 41

Lattimer, Heather, 3
learning styles, 65, 73
Lord of the Flies, viii–ix, 6–7, 9, 11, 23–24, 30, 62, 67–68, 84, 86, 91–92, 98, 100–101

main idea, 48, 54, 57, 97.
 See also key ideas and details
Marsick, Rebecca, 14
McKeown, Margaret G., 33, 39, 41
McTighe, Jay, 5
McVeigh, Timothy, vii
metacognitive development, 69
Mills, Allisyn, 7, 90
modeling, 46, 52
Moffett, James, 42–43, 85
Moon, Seungho, 7, 90
motivation, viii–ix, 9
multimedia texts, 8, 23, 71–73, 85–87;
 audio, 8, 25, 27, 66, 71–73;
 PSA, 72;
 video, 8, 23–25, 31, 66, 69, 71–73, 85
multiple-choice, 36, 51–52;
 paired questions, 38, 54, 56;
 student-generated questions, 46;
 word problems, 74

National Center on Literacy Education, 18, 18n1
NCTE, 89

The New York Times, 6, 68, 23, 25, 30, 72, 94;
    Learning Network, 24;
    Text to Text, 24

organizers, ix;
    T chart, 79

PARCC, ix, 36, 52, 56, 71, 77–79
professional development, 18, 89
prompts:
    standardized assessment-style, 77–79;
    for writing and discussion, 24, 61, 71, 85–86, 88
purpose, 5, 8–9, 33, 40, 46–48

A Raisin in the Sun, 23, 72
Rami, Meenoo, x
reflective narrative, 68–69, 101
research, 13, 27, 65, 67–69, 98, 101–102;
    databases, 24
rubrics, ix, 12, 67, 99–100, 102–103

Schwarze, Janice, 12
small-group work, 52
Smarter Balanced, ix, 36, 52, 56, 73, 77–79
standardized assessment, ix, 36, 51–54, 56, 77–81, 88;
    format, 38
Stretching Beyond the Textbook, 14
summative activity, 86

test preparation, ix, 51–52, 77–79, 87–88;
    test-taking skills, 52
text features, viii, 45, 56;
    discipline-specific, 47;

length, 29.
    See also informational text, structure of
To Kill a Mockingbird, vii–viii, 5, 14, 72
Tovani, Cris, 45, 63
TubeChop, 72
twenty-first-century skills, 13, 75

usinginformationaltext.org, ix, n18, 25, 72, 80, 100–101
Using Informational Text to Teach A Raisin in the Sun, 23
Using Informational Text to Teach To Kill a Mockingbird, vii, 72

vocabulary, viii, 17, 24, 28–29, 33–34, 45, 71, 77, 84–88, 92–94;
    academic language, 33–34;
    acquisition, 35;
    context clues, 36, 38, 40–41, 52–53, 56;
    dictionary, use of, 38–39, 41, 43;
    discipline-specific, 34, 43;
    parts of speech, 41;
    pre-reading activities, 34–35, 45–47;
    Tier Two and Three words, 44;
    vocabulary skits, 41–43, 73, 85, 93–94;
    word forms, 41, 43.
    See also multiple-choice

Wagner, Betty J., 42–43, 85
The Wall Street Journal, 25
Wessling, Sarah Brown, 4–5, 7
whole-class instruction, 52
Wiggins, Grant, 5
Wilson, Amy Alexandra, 5, 67, 75

About the Authors

Audrey Fisch is Professor of English and Coordinator of Secondary English Education at New Jersey City University where she has taught for over twenty years. She has published a wide variety of academic work (including books with Cambridge and Oxford University Presses, numerous scholarly articles, and writing about teaching). She also works as a curriculum consultant and professional development provider for K-12 districts in New Jersey.

Susan Chenelle teaches English and journalism at University Academy Charter High School in Jersey City, New Jersey, where she also serves as the English department lead and peer coach for humanities. She holds a master's degree in education from New Jersey City University and a bachelor's degree in English from Kenyon College. Previously, she was a writer and editor for ten years for publications like MSN.com and Citysearch.com.

Together, Audrey and Susan have also published *Using Informational Text to Teach to Kill a Mockingbird* (Rowman 2014) and *Using Informational Text to Teach A Raisin in the Sun* (Rowman 2016). They present their ideas about using informational text at conferences and in schools across the country.

www.ingramcontent.com/pod-product-compliance
Lightning Source LLC
Chambersburg PA
CBHW030145240426
43672CB00005B/283